FORESTRY IN SOUTHERN INDIA

FORESTRY IN SOUTHERN INDIA,

MAJOR- GENERAL H. R. MORGAN

EDITED BY

JOHN SHORTT, M.D., M.R.C.P. & S., F.L.S., &c.

GYAN

Published by

Gyan Publishing House
5, Ansari Road
Daryaganj, New Delhi-110002
Phone: 011-47034999, 9811692060
E-mail: books@gyanbooks.com

Distribution Network
gyanbooks.com
India, USA, Canada, UK, Australia, France

ISBN: 978-81-212-9296-2 (PB)
First Published, 1884

2nd Impression 2023

Printed at: Gyan Press, Delhi.

FORESTRY IN SOUTHERN INDIA
Author: H. R. MORGAN, Editor: JOHN SHORTT

FORESTRY IN SOUTHERN INDIA,

BY

MAJOR-GENERAL H. R. MORGAN,

LATE DEPUTY CONSERVATOR OF FORESTS, MADRAS.

EDITED BY

JOHN SHORTT, M.D., M.R.C.P. & S., F.L.S., &c.,

RETIRED DEPUTY SURGEON-GENERAL, MADRAS ARMY.

MADRAS:

HIGGINBOTHAM AND CO.

By Appointment in India to His Royal Highness the Prince of Wales,
and Publishers to the Madras University.

1884.

PREFACE.

HAVING for nearly twenty years been employed either in working or inspecting the working of forests for Government, I may claim to have had some experience in forest matters. I am aware that there is yet much to be learnt in the working of our forests and in the conservancy of the same. Hitherto there has been no manual on these subjects to guide the young Forest Officer. Hints lie scattered here and there in the various Forest Reports. I have, therefore, put together the result of my twenty years' experience, in the hope that they may be useful, though imperfect. I have selected the forests of Nellumboor, Wynaad and Anamullies, as they are, the forests principally worked for Teak, and are at the same time those with which I am most familiar. The remaining forests in this Presidency have hitherto been worked on the License and Voucher system, and do not afford scope for remark. I have cited no authorities to support my statement as there are none.

A short time ago the acquirements expected of an officer in the Salt Department were enumerated, so multifarious were they that they even transcended the knowledge demanded from a Forest Officer if possible, and these are not trifling when I mention that a Forest Officer to be really useful should know first and foremost the language of the people, without this he is useless, or at best, at the mercy of intriguing interpreters in addition to the language, the habits and customs of the people, then Arboriculture in all its branches, next Engineering and Surveying—how to build houses and bridges, survey roads, and blocks of forest, &c., run boundaries by a pickaxe trench, and mounds of earth, stones are useless. Physic his people when ill, treat them with tact, attend to the health of his bullocks and elephants, and last but not least, keep his own health, answer endless letters, and understand accounts. The life of a Forest Officer is not cast on a bed of roses, but rather a bed of thorns, an iron constitution and a good conscience may enable him to surmount all his difficulties, and wishing him the possession of all these priceless gifts, I subscribe myself,

AN OLD FOREST OFFICER.

INTRODUCTION.

The Teak tree scientifically known as the *Tectona grandis* belongs to the natural order of Verbenaceæ or Vervain order, a genus of dicotyledonous plants deriving its name from the Indian one of *tekka* or *theka* used to designate the principal species. The most important, if not the only species, is the Tectona grandis, a large tree, a native of India, the wood of which is well known by the name of Teak or *Sagwān*. It is hard, and durable, and of great use in building ships as well as for many other useful purposes, as it is very hard and of longer duration than the oak. It is often called the Indian Oak, having ashy-coloured and scaly bark with the young shoots, four-sided and grooved without stipules, large deciduous leaves measuring from twelve to twenty-four inches long, and from eight to sixteen inches broad, rough and covered with short stiff hairs above, whitish and downy beneath, panicles terminal, large cross-armed divided in twos with a stemless fertile flower in each cleft or division covered with a brown mealy powder, and the stalks are deeply grooved with four prominent angles, and flowers numerous small white, the outer and inner envelopes, five to six cleft, stamens, six, ovary round hairy, four-celled cells, one seeded nut very hard. It flowers in June and July, and the seeds ripen in September and October.

Dye.—From the tender leaves a purple colour is extracted which is used as a dye for silk and cotton cloths.

Medicinal.—The young leaves are eaten boiled with sugar in sore mouth, and the flowers prepared much in the same way in dropsy. The green fruits are compounded into an ointment and used for various skin eruptions.

Wood.—The timber which is hard but light is easily worked, and is soon seasoned from being oily, it does not shrink nor injure iron, and resists the attacks of white ants and other insects on land, and the *Laminora terebrans* or other crustaceæ when exposed to the action of the sea-water. It weighs when seasoned about forty-seven pounds the cubic foot. Of the different localities in which it grows, Malabar Teak is considered the best and most valuable, whilst the greatest quantity is obtained from Pegu, the price varies from three to five rupees the cubic foot, and it is the most useful, strong and valuable timber met with in India; occasionally specimens may be seen beautifully veined and mottled. In about twenty-five years the stem attains a diameter of two feet, but to attain maturity, it takes from fifty to one hundred years, attaining an enormous size. The Teak is found growing in the Southern and Western parts of the peninsular of India, in Malabar, Canara, Wynaad, Anamallies, Burmah, Sumatra, Java, Cutches and Sumatra, Upper Godavery and Central Provinces.

CONTENTS.

CHAPTER I.

TEAK FORESTS.

Page.

CHAPTER II.

MANAGEMENT OF TEAK FORESTS.

ERRATA.

PAGE.

30 line 19 *for* Malabar *read* Mysore.

42 „ 19 „ cutch *read* Dye wood.

54 (margin) *for* fradinifolia *read* fraxinifolia.

54 „ „ munricata *read* muricata.

55 „ „ Camphora officinarum *read* Dryabalanops Camphora.

56 „ „ Sterculia foetida *read* Callophyllum angustifolium.

60 line 15 *after* Queensland *strike out* Hill.

73 „ 26 for *Jannesabit* read *Jamboolana.*

81 last para. *from* After the whole, &c., *to* with new species, on page 98 belongs to Fuel Plantations by Rhodes Morgan, and should be added on to page 140.

FORESTRY IN SOUTHERN INDIA.

CHAPTER I.

ON THE MANAGEMENT OF TEAK FORESTS.

On first taking over a Teak forest it is well to ascertain the probable amount of ripe trees contained in the square mile, an acre is no criterion at all, even a square mile will only be a very approximate estimate, for Teak being gregarious, one square mile may contain a thousand trees or more, and then for five square miles, you may hardly find a single tree. The reason is this. The seed is a heavy one, and eaten by no birds; squirrels occasionally carry a seed a few yards to a neighbouring tree to devour it, and the Teak is spread for a small area around the parent tree. Rains too wash the seed down into hollows where it may germinate, but as a rule the Teak trees in a forest increase very slowly, and to trust to nature alone is a fallacy. Though no birds eat the Teak seed, there are hundreds of rats and squirrels in the forest, quite enough to eat up every Teak seed that falls.* I have examined thousands of Teak seeds in the forest, and as a rule have found the mark of the squirrels or rats' teeth. The Teak seed is peculiar—it has two to four cells encased in a hard shell, each cell has a little trap-door, which, on lifting with a penknife, discloses the kernel. Though every seed may have four cells, they are not always full, for sometimes only one germinates, but often two, rarely three, and scarcely ever four. Sometimes the squirrel or rat eats the contents of one or two cells, and leaves one intact, this may or may not germinate. But it is clear from the havoc committed by these four-footed vermin that

Ripe trees.

Nature of Teak seed.

Rats and squirrels.

Form of Teak seed.

* Brown of Arniston could not sow acorns on account of mice and rats, &c, page 357.

the seed has a small chance, and very little is gained by shutting up teak forests so far as the germination of seed is concerned and the increase of young plants. It is not so with other trees, for instance, the Sal seed germinates in the air sometimes, and its vitality is small—this is why Sal trees are gregarious, and when fires are kept out, they spring up in thousands, whereas in walking through a Teak forest for a whole day, you will hardly see hundreds of Teak saplings.

Shutting of Teak forest.

Sal seeds germinate at once.

Amount of annual yield.

Having ascertained what amount of ripe timber your forest is likely to yield and the market demand, you must cut accordingly. Let us assume that your demand is fifty thousand cubic feet annually, and that your forest is capable of supplying that amount for thirty years. It becomes evident that you must plant to supply the deficiency. It is but of little use scattering seed here and there in the hopes of its growing, the cost, it is true, is not much, but then the returns are almost nil. There is one way in which seed may be made use of, (though even that is doubtful, as rats have a very keen scent, and are apt to dig up the seed;) when it is impossible, on account of the area or unhealthiness of the locality to form a regular plantation, then the following system can be tried. The seeds in May may be soaked for twenty-four hours in warm water, then buried in sand in a heap, and left to germinate.

Scattering seed no use.

Sowing seed.

When the shoot appears, the men proceed to the selected spot, having previously made holes with crow-bars at six feet intervals—the holes to be six inches deep, and enlarged at the top by working the crow-bar about, one man fills in the holes to within an inch of the top, the next man places a germinated seed in the hole, the third man covers it up. In this manner a small party of men may, in a season between June and August, plant up an area of some ninety acres. Four men should hole an acre with one thousand holes and four men plant it. It is probable that on account of the number of trees already occupying the ground, that not more than five hundred seeds could be put in, should there be any Teak trees on the ground, it will be useless planting near them, indeed a radius of thirty feet should be kept clear. In selecting a piece of ground for planting up with Teak, it will be advisable not to have too many Teak trees on it. It will also be well to clear it of bushes, and to make the holes when the ground is free from grass, before putting in the crow-bar, it will be best if there is grass, to cut out a sod a foot square, to prevent the grass from strangling the young plants. A square block is best to select as more easily watched. A fire-path should be cut round it at least six feet wide and fire rigidly kept out, for, should the young plant survive an attack of fire, the disease of heartshake is established, and it is the constant forest fires that cause heartshake by damaging the young saplings. Fire-path.

As most of our Teak forests consist of one to two hundred square miles, it is obvious that the area to be supervised being so enormous, the planting requires to be concentrated as much as possible, and in selecting blocks for planting up, it is best to have a regard to facilities of carriage by water or by land. Carriage facilities.

Assuming that we do not rely altogether on germinated seed, but resolve to form a regular plantation, to replace the annual demand, for timber, we select a block of land that is accessible by road or water—and the soil and climate suitable—for it often happens that the eastern end of a forest may be dry and the soil indifferent, and the western though, only ten miles distant, possesses a different climate and soil, in fact both suitable for Teak growing, the only drawback being the extra cost of carriage. It is far better to pay the extra cost rather than have an indifferent plantation. As shown above, the demands are fifty thousand cubic feet annually. We must, therefore, plant a sufficient area to produce something more than that amount annually at the end of thirty years. The annual increase of Teak may be taken in a favorable situation at one cubic foot a year. At Nellumbore it is over two cubic feet annually. That is a tree forty years old will have forty cubic feet of marketable Sites. Growth of Teak.

timber if properly trained. Teak trees, if well planted and pruned, can be drawn up to sixty and seventy feet without a branch. This is done first by close planting, second by pruning, if you plant six by six and thin out at the twelfth year always presuming that your trees have grown fast, then you will secure a good straight growth.

There is but little demand in India for curved timber, consequently to prevent loss and waste it is essential to secure straight growth. The best soil for a Teak plantation is a sandy clay on the banks of a stream, the ground should slope gently towards the stream, if too steep, the soil on the top of the hill is apt to be indifferent. There are other soils such as a brown surface soil with a rather retentive sub-soil of yellow clay, in such a place Teak grows well.

Soils.

From Mudumalli in the south to the end of the Wynaad Forests in the north there are thousands of acres suitable for planting. In Wynaad there is water carriage from the Cubbany river to near Mysore. In Mudumalli at a distance of some ten miles is the high road to Mysore. In the Anamullies the soil and climate are well suited for the growth of Teak, and numerous sites could be chosen; at Nellumbore there are still some five thousand acres suitable for Teak plantations. In fact if Teak planting was pursued with energy at the rate of one thousand acres a year, there is sufficient land to occupy the Forest Department in planting for the next century and more. There is but little Teak in Madura or Tinnevelly, and there must be some suitable sites in those localities. Teak, it will be observed, grows at the sea-level, the foot of the Carcoor Ghât near Nellumbore is only five hundred feet above the sea, and it grows well on some of the hills in Wynaad over three thousand feet in elevation, given a fair soil and plenty of moisture, Teak grows well, but does not stand drying easterly winds. When inexperienced people see Teak that has been cut over, and throwing up large shoots with large leaves, they imagine at once that the soil and climate are suitable for Teak and that some primeval forest of Teak once existed and had been

Locality for sites.

utterly destroyed; the truth being that both soil and climate were incapable of producing good Teak, and at the best stunted specimens grew there which never contained five cubic feet of marketable timber, a notable example may be found in the Hills near Cuddapah, and Mr. E. C. Thomas, c. s., in his work "Famine" alludes to the Teak trees there as once a fine forest and cites the size of the leaves on the shoots as a criterion of the magnitude of the trees. There is another example, near Musnacoil at the foot of the Segoor Ghât, hundreds of Teak trees are seen bordering the road with leaves as large as the finest trees have in a good forest, and yet those trees have never produced, and never will produce five cubic feet of good timber. Yet ten miles west as the crow flies, fine Teak will be found, so great, an alteration of climate does ten miles produce in this locality whereas ten miles further west in the Cuddapah jungles would produce no change whatsoever. We will suppose that in your forest of one to two hundred square miles, you have plenty of blank spaces to fill in, some you devote to the planting of germinated seed, but in more favorable localities such as when there is good soil, easy carriage by road or water, a scarcity of Teak, you determine upon a regular plantation of at least five hundred acres to be planted at the rate of twenty acres a year; this will meet the loss of the fifty thousand cubic feet taken out annually, by this process, in a few years, you have provided for a demand in future years much in excess of present requirements. As a Teak tree in fair localities may be supposed to make a cubic foot a year, at the end of thirty years your acre will represent two hundred trees containing at least six thousand cubic feet of good timber, half of these are cut out representing three thousand cubic feet. The remaining hundred may be left to stand for another thirty years, by which time they will average sixty cubic feet each or six thousand cubic feet in all. These nine thousand cubic feet should represent at least 9,000 rupees. In addition to this, I allow nothing for the trees taken out between twelve and thirty years of age though as poles it would be found that

Teak plantation.

they brought a remunerative price. The account would stand thus:—

	RS.	A.	P.
To felling and clearing 20 acres at 15 Rs....	300	0	0
1,200 pits 18″ at 10 Rs. per 1,000	240	0	0
Planting per acre at 6 Rs.	120	0	0
Cost of plants per acre at 6 Rs.	120	0	0
Weeding first year, 5 Rs. per acre	100	0	0
	880	0	0
Supervision ten per cent.	88	0	0
Rs.	968	0	0

1st year—

Felling and clearing 20 acres at 15 Rs. ...	300	0	0
1,200 plants per acre at 6 Rs.	120	0	0
1,200 pits at 12 Rs.	240	0	0
Planting per acre 6 Rs.	120	0	0
Weeding 1st year at 5 Rs.	100	0	0
Rs.	880	0	0
Supervision 10 per cent	88	0	0
	968	0	0
Tools	200	0	0
	1,168	0	0
Weeding 12 years at 100 Rs. a year ...	1,200	0	0
	2,368	0	0
Interest 5 per cent. 12 years...	1,416	0	0
	3,784	0	0
Cutting 10,000 trees at 25 Rs. per 1,000 ...	384	0	0
Supervision 12 years at 40 Rs. a year ...	480	0	0
Rs.	4,648	0	0

For this year 1882, Teak is selling in Madras for 2-8-0 to 3-8-0 the cubic foot, and to carry Teak from Wynaad to Madras costs as follows :—

	RS.	A.	P.
Floating to Nungengode per ton of fifty cubic feet	6	0	0
Carting to Railway Mysore	2	0	0
Rail, Mysore to Madras 280 miles, 8 pie a ton a mile	12	0	0
Carting to Depôt	2	0	0
If we add 3 Rs. for agency charges *en route* and at Madras	3	0	0
Rs.	25	0	0

We have a total charge of 8 annas a cubic foot added to total value in Forest one rupee makes the wood delivered in Madras 1-8 0 per cubic foot.

From Nellumbore and the Anamallies, the cost would be about the same. Let us take Nellumbore :—

Floating or carriage by steamer per ton to Beypore	6	0	0
Rail to Madras 8 pie per ton per mile 400 miles	16	10	0
Carting to Depôt	2	0	0
Cost of agency per ton	3	0	0
Rs.	27	0	0

This is a little over 1-8-0 per cubic foot.

From the Anamallies the cost would be—

Carting to Coimbatore per ton say	6	0	0
Railfare to Madras 300 miles	12	0	0
Carting to Depôt	2	0	0
Agency, &c.	3	0	0
Rs.	23	0	0

This shows a little under 1-8-0 per cubic foot. It has always appeared to me that if the Forest officer had an efficient establishment, his duty was to carry his timber to the best market, for merchants dislike going into feverish forests, the risk is too great, consequently when they do go, the revenue suffers. It is always easier for the Forest Department to undertake work in the forest than outsiders always assuming that the establishment is a strong one. I have no hesitation in saying that the revenue of the forests, *viz.*, Wynaad, Anamallies, and Nellumbore might have been doubled if efficient establishments both for the conservation and working of the forests had been kept up from the formation of the department. Unfortunately a revenue was demanded at once, and the result was that conservancy had to be abandoned. In addition to this there was no Forest law, damage by cattle and fires were a bar to all improvements; convictions could not be obtained, some Collectors were in favor of conserving the forests strictly, others the reverse. A Forest officer had no sooner established an understanding with the Collector and got things to work amicably than there came another Collector who had quite different views and ideas, and everything went to ruin. One Member of Council was in favour of shutting up the Anamallies, another was not, and so the matter went on until what ought to have been an admirable department storing up the sources of a large revenue for future years, became like a certain other department, not a saving department but a spending one.

Forest establishment.

Forest law.

No Forest policy.

Forest staff.

As every forest is now to have a strong staff backed up by a Forest law, there will be some chance of forestry in Madras, being placed in a safe position for the future; but five and twenty years have been lost, and it will take very heavy efforts to recover only a portion of the ground.

It is satisfactory to know that one part of the Forest Department has not been suffered to languish, and that is the Teak planting of Nellumboro. With over 3,000 acres planted and some 5,000 acres still to plant up,—there is work cut out here for many a day.

I had since 1860 been more or less connected with these splendid plantations until I retired from the service in 1874, when working the Mudumalli Forest for the Wellington Barracks which I was engaged in building, I had occasion in 1857 to visit the Rajah of Nellumbore about forest matters, and first saw the Teak plantations then about thirteen years old—in 1860, I visited them officially and found that the 1845 plantation had never been thinned, and required to be operated upon at once. The 1843 and 44 plantations had been thinned more by failures than by the hand of man—they were poor and of no extent; but the 1845 was a very fine one, and the old Overseer Chatoo Menon could not bring himself to cut out the trees. I had to mark the trees myself and followed by half a dozen axe-men, in a week we had made a considerable gap, and the ice once broken, the old man went on thinning out under the auspices of Overseer Hall whom I sent down to assist him. This 1845 block should have been thinned three years before, the trees were crowding each other and making no progress.

Nellumbore Teak plantations.

Management.

Thinning.

In 1860 I was enabled to appoint Mr. Ferguson to the charge of these important plantations, and Chatoo Menon retired on a pension which he had well earned. Here I must record how faithfully and how well this native had served the Government; connected with the Nellumbore Rajah's family, he had position, and being immediately under the orders of the Collector, he, of course, derived considerable support from the Revenue authorities. From 1843 to 1860 Chatoo Menon had been incessantly engaged in planting, and had put out about a million of Teak plants on 1,200 acres. Mr. Ferguson, a practical Forester, soon mastered the details of planting and pruning, and when I saw the 1845 plantation in 1872, the trees were about seventy feet high and fifty feet without a branch,—they were then nearly thirty years old, and had then over fifty cubic feet of

Chatoo Menon.

Mr. Ferguson.

1845 trees.

timber in them. They have now over one hundred cubic feet in 1883.

At Nellumbore it was remarkable to see how enormous was the growth of the trees on the river banks, and how the size gradually receded to one-third on the tops of the low Hills especially where laterite cropped out on the surface showing of what vital importance is good soil

Size of trees on River banks.

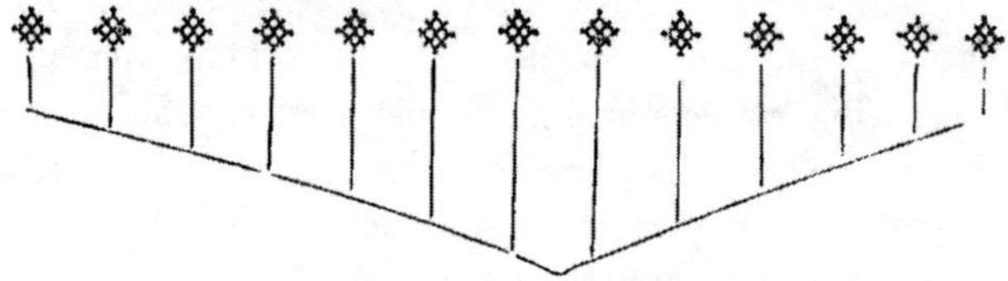

to a Teak plantation. It may here be remarked that on the banks of rivers in this locality, the soil is of a rather sandy clay, easily penetrated by the roots and fully drained, inland the sub-soil is often composed of soft laterite, but where it comes to the surface and is hardened by the action of the air, the trees almost refused to grow. The usual soil in Wynaad is a very dark brown surface soil with rather a dark yellow sub-soil, in this Teak grows well, for, like the oak, it has no objection to a clay sub-soil.

Soils, sub-soils.

Fastgrowing timber.

Lindley has laid down that fast growing timber is the best, and so far as my experience enables me to judge I agree with him. About the year 1872 Colonel Beddome reported to Government that he did not think the Nellumbore plantations would last, several fine trees had died in an unaccountable manner, and some appeared stag-headed. He thought the climate too forcing, and was doubtful about the success of the experiment. Shortly after this he was obliged to proceed to Australia for his health, and I took up his duties. At the same time Government requested me to report upon the state of the Nellumbore plantations. I accordingly visited them, and in company with Mr. Ferguson, who was in charge, examined the dead trees. I could find no trace of unsoundness in the timber, but I did detect mycelium at the roots which fully accounted for the trees dying. The cause as explained by Mr. Ferguson I agreed in, *viz.*, the trees were situated on a flat close to the bank of a large stream which had overflowed, and the trees remained under water for some months. This caused disease at the roots, they died, and of course the trees died.

With regard to the stag-headed appearance of some of the trees, I could only account for it by supposing that Colonel Beddome had seen them early in the year when perhaps some of the ends of the top-most branches had not developed their leaves, or from being struck by lightening for I could not find a single stag-headed tree. On going over the ground, I saw a number of fine Teak logs on the ground, and on enquiry was shown the stumps from which they had been cut, on examination of the logs, I counted seventy rings, and the stumps showed plainly that this was a second growth, and the conclusion I arrived at was that the stump was not less than one hundred and fifty years old, and might, from its healthy appearance, produce another shoot equal to what it had already done—as this was natural Teak growing close to a plantation, it became evident that the soil and climate was quite capable of producing very large trees, and that they would be healthy certainly up to one hundred and fifty years of age, and probably to two hundred and fifty years; and I have not the slightest hesitation in saying that I consider the Nellumbore Teak plantations capable of enduring for centuries.

Col. Beddome's Report on the plantations.

My report on the plantations.

Cause of disease.

Age of Teak trees on the land.

Suitable climate and soil.

In forming a Teak plantation in forest land, of course, every jungle tree is cut over, and then burnt, or if any of the timber is valuable, it is first cut out and dragged to a convenient distance away from fire. If felling is commenced in October, the wood will burn well in March, in April, the ground should be lined out and pitted, the holes to be 18″ cubic, and six feet by six feet. In collecting seed in November and December, great care should be used to prevent seed being taken from stunted weakly trees, as it is so much easier to gather from such than from tall trees,—no seed should be picked up from the ground, as the chances are

Forming a plantation.

Felling, pitting.

Treatment of seed.

that squirrels and rats have already attacked them. When the seed is gathered, it is tied up in bundles of grass, and kept in a dry place free from rats. In April your seed-beds having been made close to water, and slightly raised some four inches with raised edges to retain water. The seed is soaked for twenty-four hours in warm water,—it may then be kept for ten days in a heap mixed with damp sand, it is

Seed-beds.

then planted in beds in lines six inches apart in the rows. The beds are then covered over with grass to keep in the moisture, and are saturated with water of an evening daily,

Treatment of seed. See Forest Report, 1871-72, page 9.

directly one or two seeds show above ground, it is time to remove the grass. In Nellumbore by June the plants are six inches high, they are then carefully lifted out of the bed line by line, their tap roots cut back to four inches, and then they are put out in the pits. In Wynaad where the climate is much colder, the seeds sometimes do not

Climate, Wynaad and Nellumbore.

show above ground for six weeks, and are not fit to be put out before August, hence it is necessary to germinate them in heaps. The difference of elevation some three thousand feet makes the weather 10 degrees colder than Nellumbore, at

Growth of trees.

this place the growth of young plants is very rapid, the leaves are soon so large, that they shade the ground, and keep the roots cool in the hot weather. I may say that in the first year the trees at Nellumbore grow twice as fast as those in the Wynaad. It is a good plan to dip the roots of the young plants in a mixture of clay and cow-dung made into a thin paste. When the young plants are established, little remains to be done, beyond keeping them

Thinning out.

fairly clean and reducing two stems to one. Pruning is never required until the first thinning of the plantation, so to save this expensive business, the trees have purposely been planted six by six. Thus they cover the ground, prevent weeds, and do not throw out lateral branches. In the twelfth year, if the trees require room, as a rule, about one-half are taken out, great care being used to select the weakest trees—of course, if in one place, you find three or four strong trees together, some must come out, but thinning really requires some knowledge, and it is not to be left to unskilful hands. I have heard of all the strong trees being taken out to let the weakly ones come on, it need scarcely be observed that such a course of action is sufficient to ruin any timber plantation. In a Forest Report, of the Pegue Forests, 1856, it is recommended to plant Teak in rows from eight to fifteen feet apart, and two to three feet in the rows. The reasons given are that the rows being fifteen feet apart plants have ample room to extend their foliage, also any other system does not permit trees of a naturally stronger constitution than the rest to develop themselves freely on account of their being surrounded on all sides by other trees.

Planting Teak rows not suitable.

The Nellumbore plantation gives the denial to this.

Now, I most certainly cannot agree in this opinion, for to draw up trees and escape pruning is the end and aim of our planting, to obtain marketable timber, planting close must be the rule. It is not argued that if crooked timber is required that plants fifteen feet apart in the rows would be a mistake, certainly not, for it may safely be assumed that more than half the timber grown in this fashion would be curved. The waste in the forests from the curved state of the stems of natural grown Teak is enormous, and this waste we wish to avoid. The writer also falls into another mistake—he writes, page 52, "The general opinion in India is against planted Teak." Now this was written in 1856 when the Conelly Teak Plantations at Nellumbore had been in existence since 1843 or thirteen years. The fact is that in later years Forest officers could not obtain money for planting. In 1860 I recommended to Government that every Forest officer should be passed through Nellumbore that he might learn practical planting on a large scale, and I believe three or four Forest officers were sent to Nellumbore. With regard to planting and forestry in India, it may here be remarked that the European Forester has much to unlearn. Mr. Ferguson found a system already adopted and succeeding admirably, so he had nothing to do, but follow in the footsteps of his predecessor so far as planting went.

Wastes in forests of curved Teak.

Planting the rule in S. India

Officers to study at Nellumbore.

European forestry not suited to India.

The pruning, of course, was his own idea, and he found

Pruning not to be delayed.

that by pruning early, he not only saved himself much trouble but the trees never felt it. It is a fatal thing to delay pruning, it cannot be taken in hand too soon after the first thinning. A fine straight stem of forty feet having been secured, but little pruning after that is required.

Never cut into the stem.

It is understood that in pruning to cut back a large branch into the stem of the tree is fatal, as rot surely takes place, and a severe wound in the stem is the consequence, should a large branch, say, over three inches in diameter, require amputating, it is better to shorten it at a distance of two or three feet from the stem rather than cut it off close to the tree. It is sometimes necessary to cut a branch clean off, in such a case assuming the tree to be a valuable one, it is advisable to dress the surface of the wound with a mixture of clay and cow-dung, but such a plan could not be adopted in large plantations, and is only brought forward here as an extreme case.

Dressing wounds.

Working the forest.

Fences no use against elephants and bison.

Enemies of young trees.

Time for felling.

Depôts.

It may sometimes happen that the leader is lost early, in which case two leaders appear, one must be shortened to two feet. We must now assume that the planting of the forest, both by germinated seed and by young plants, is progressing favorably, that fire-paths have been cut and cattle carefully kept out, a fence is of but little use against elephants and bison, as a rule, they do not do much damage, but sambur and spotted deer are in the habit, when the trees are young, of barking them severely, shooting them is the only cure. All these matters having been arranged, we now proceed to the felling operations. These must only be carried on during the wane of the moon for seven days in the last quarter, and in the months of November, December, January and February, as in those months the sap is down, and if the timber is cut at the wane of the moon, it seasons readily; the timber can be squared during the rest of the month. As fast as the timber is squared, it should be dragged to a Depôt close to the main road and stacked. The Depôt to be carefully fire-traced, even this will not always avail, for on one occasion over 20,000 Rupees of timber was burnt on the Anamallies in the following manner: It appeared that a very large quantity of Teak leaves was driven by wind against the stack of timber and lodged there; when the forest was on fire, sparks caught the inflammable Teak leaves, and these being set a light, communicated fire to the stack. No one found it out for two or three days when the alarm was given, the Forest officer was miles away, water was not available, and the huge stack of timber burnt on. It was specially fine timber, having been selected for the building of a frigate, and the loss was great. At last the Forest officer arrived, and by means of his elephants, put out the fire by burying the ends of the logs in the ground. The experience obtained by the fire was, always burn the grass for two hundred yards round your Depôt, never leave more than one hundred logs in one place. The Depôts may be two hundred yards apart. Teak on fire never flares up, it simply smoulders slowly, so if it catches fire, by burying the end in earth and excluding the air, the fire is soon put out. I have often seen sparks carried two and three hundred yards in a fierce wind. In constructing a main road through a forest, it is advisable to have it on easy gradients, with many feeders, it must always be borne in mind that dragging costs more than carting, in fact your dragging should never cost more than one anna a cubic foot, for instance, if you cut fifty thousand cubic feet in a year, the cost of your elephants should not exceed 3,125 Rupees per annum, and as every elephant costs at least 60 Rupees a month, five elephants should suffice, but if you drag where you should cart, two annas a cubic foot will not be enough. In making your bridges, it is advisable to have the abutments of rough stone and kura murra* beams laid across, and over them a bamboo mat.

Burning of Teak Depôt, Anamallies.

Distance of Depôts from each other.

How to put out fire.

Main Road.

Dragging.

Bridges.

Elephants should not be allowed over bridges, nor should they be allowed on the main roads in wet weather, as a full grown elephant weighs five tons, and they cut up the roads dreadfully. Wild elephants frequently destroy forest bridges. If they (Forest elephants,) must go on the main road, the banks of the stream should be sloped down on both sides to

---

* Terminalia coriacea.

avoid passing over the bridges. In the hot weather, your bridges must be protected from fire. In fact what with floods floating away your bridge beams, wild elephants pulling them down, and fire getting in, bridges perpetually require repair; fortunately, in most of all the forests, kura murra is plentiful and makes splendid bridges up to twenty-five feet span. If the stone abutments are fairly well built, they should last a long time.

Main Roads

Forest roads are only meant for carting over in the dry weather, so the carting should all be done in about six months.

Carting.

It will be advisable to have your own carts for work in the forest. The wheels and axles should be extra strong, capable of carrying three tons, as the jars to which the axles are subjected in rough forest roads is very considerable. It is a good plan to have the wheels and axles made up in a large town. The poles can be got in the forest, they are made of kura murra. The beams are slung under the pole, and axle beam by means of chains, the weight being very low down within two feet of the ground, upsets are not common, four bullocks will take a ton of timber over rough forest roads with ease. It is always advisable to keep your roads in as good order as possible; a few hundreds of rupees carefully laid out in repair is a good investment.

Mode of dragging.

In dragging timber, I am entirely in favor of harness. It is true that sometimes, from the Mahout, not looking to the stuffing of the collar, a swelling is caused in the point of the shoulder which requires to be opened, and the animal may be laid up for a month or more, but it is invariably the fault of the Mahout. The swelling chiefly occurs in elephants new to the work.

On the Anamallies the elephant drags by the teeth, so they do in many parts of Malabar. It is a most pernicious practice, because it loosens the teeth, and an elephant's grinders once out of order, he has to be laid up for a long time before he recovers. I am aware that the elephants do not entirely depend on their teeth, but assist themselves by means of their trunks, still they cannot always avoid heavy jars.

The Mahouts are very fond of giving raw rice or paddy to elephants, the result is that much is stolen, and much passes through the animal undigested. To obviate this, there are two courses—one is the Burmah custom of giving baked cakes of rice, the other, the one I always pursued in the forest, was to damp the paddy for three days till it germinated exactly as barley is malted for beer. I found my elephants kept in better condition on thirty pounds of dry paddy, treated in this way than on forty pounds given unmalted. Mahouts are very fond of asking for *massala* for elephants and of doctoring them, some of them are skilful in curing wounds of the feet, or sores on the back and shoulders. Elephants are subject to worms, and frequently eat mud as the Mahouts phrase is "*Mutteekhàia hei*"—the fact is the elephant delights in a salt lick, quite as much as a deer, and should have salt in his food frequently, the Mahouts never give it if they can help it. They prefer that their elephants should be laid up for two or three days after eating mud. In wet weather elephants should have massala, and if possible be kept under cover at night.

Elephants' food.

Medicinal as well for worms.

This is natural when they eat mud.

Male elephants should be worked regularly, or when old, they are certain to get Must, and every succeeding fit, is worse than the last, until they become quite useless; to prevent this, regular work, with a diminution of food, has a good effect. In dragging timber, rollers are rarely used, but in some places, they are of immense use saving the elephant and rendering the transport of huge beams possible. I have seen three elephants harnessed to a log, and unable to move it, simply because rollers were not used. A powerful elephant will drag fifty cubic feet of timber over level ground, but when it comes to dragging over hills and swamps, he cannot manage more than thirty feet, and even that with difficulty. In fact Mahouts should be cautioned not to strain their charges up steep hills or down them. A Commissariat male, I was once working, in going down a hill, the beam took a sudden slide between his legs, after that he became frightened and refused to do a stroke of work. I never could make out if it was not a trick of the

Must in elephants, treatment of.

Rollers for dragging.

Mahouts.

Mahouts as Commissariat Mahouts, as a rule, are quite worthless in the jungles, they infinitely prefer the distractions of the bazaar. Extra batta was not a sufficient bait to keep them straight, indeed forest Mahouts are, as a rule, an inferior set of men, given to bhang and other abominations.

Nature of elephants.

Elephants differ as much as horses in shape, muscular power, temper, and constitution. The Burmah ones are very good, those caught in Southern India generally fairly good; but Ceylon elephants are undersized, ill-made, and weakly animals. A fair sized female, of Southern India, will be about seven to eight feet in height, and a male, eight and a half to nine feet.

Wounds of feet.

The diseases of elephants fairly fed and worked are not many. They are very apt to get wounded in the sole of the foot when dragging timber by sharp splinters of bamboo, but they are very docile, and submit to be doctored by their Mahouts readily.

Wounds or sores are readily cured by carbolic acid; to prevent worms, give salt; in wet weather, give massala, or a mixture of pepper and ginger sprinkled over the food, or if a stimulating food is required, then give five pounds daily of the following cattle food:

	Rs.	cwt.	qrs.	lbs.
Oilcake, such as cocoanut, gingelly or ground nut	21	7	...	...
Carob beans	40	8	...	...
Indian corn, cholum, raggy or gram	10	4	1	...
Powdered turmeric	6	...	1	...
Ginger	1	...	...	3
Fennygreek seed or vendium gentian...	2	...	...	10
Cream of tartar	1	...	...	10
Sulphur	5	...	...	10
Common salt...	1/8	...	...	20
Coriander	/14	...	...	7
	Rs. 88-6-0		one Ton.	

This condimental food only costs 4-8-0 a cwt., and in wet weather would be found most excellent for elephants and bullocks. When the grasses are young also, and very full of sap, cattle are apt to purge from there being no salts in the grasses; at such times condimental food is essential to keep the animals in health. Three or four pounds daily or more for elephants have a great result. As bullocks must be kept in the forest, it is of importance to keep them in health, the gram for them should always be pounded, or in wet weather, they pass it whole, whether you give boiled gram or soaked gram, pound it. I prefer soaked gram treated as the barley, *viz.*, germinated, then pounded. It is of the utmost importance to keep your animals in good condition, unless closely supervised; the Mahout and bullock-drivers starve their animals, and the work of the forest comes to a dead lock. On the subject of saw-mills, I can only refer the Saw-mills. reader to Major Campbell Walker's work, "Reports on Forest management in Europe." I have no faith in elaborate arrangements within the forests. The fever and other drawbacks soon render any machinery useless. In North Canara where elaborate arrangements were made for the introduction of the sawing machinery, the Engineer, soon after arrival, died, what has happened to the scheme, I have not been able to learn, but so long ago as 1860 I was consulted about machinery driven by water-power, and I was against it for the following reasons:—

1*st.* Any skilled labor would be very liable to be lost through fever.

2*nd.* That sawing Teak, and sawing deal were two very different matters, that it was very easy for an American to go into forests with a saw on his shoulder, set up his mill Saw-mills. in the forest, and saw away any amount of wood, having no fear of fever before his eyes, but with Teak it was different, the wood was not only very much harder than deal, but was full of oil, the hardness of the wood caused the saw to buckle, the oil clogged the saw. Mr. Groves, who had a circular saw driven by water-power in the Segoor forest, was obliged to drive his saw very slowly, or he got no work done; again, on account of fever, his men were perpetually laid up, and he had to sharpen his saws himself, a very fatiguing operation, his saws buckled if he did not closely superintend the work, and to straighten a circular saw, requires some skill. It was always my opinion that the Forest officer and his establishment had quite enough to do to work the forest in the roughest manner. Even if establishments were doubled, they will be sufficiently occupied with planting, supplying the market demands, and conservancy generally. Allowing for fever and its concomitant evils, there will never be more than one-half the establishment at work all the year round.

Fever and other drawbacks.

At one time I was very anxious to obtain a small portable saw-mill that could be set up in any part of the forests, and simply cut a beam in half longitudinally, as sometimes, I have had over thirty beams in one spot, each over sixty cubic feet that required to be reduced before they could be got out of the forest, and was obliged to employ sawyers, as it was not possible to obtain a portable Sawing Machine. The sawyers, what with fever and advances, gave endless trouble as they worked in a set of three, if one man was ill, the other two were idle, and, of course, got into debt, and all work was at a dead lock. There are many trees in Wynaad and the Anamallies which measure over sixty cubic feet, and to cut them in half (say they are thirty feet long) is to ruin them for large spans so much required in engineering works, but this was found to be the common custom in Wynaad under the Assistants; in spite of orders to the contrary which were to keep logs up to forty cubic feet intact. A fifteen-foot log represented a cart-load, and so they cut them to that length, thus reducing the value of the timber to one-half.

CHAPTER II.

MANAGEMENT OF TEAK FORESTS—(*continued.*)

Wellington Barrack's timber supply.

WHEN I was sent up specially to build the Wellington Barracks, in 1856, I found they had no timber on hand, and could only obtain a small supply from the Anamallies with difficulty at an immense cost, for it was carted up the old Coonoor Ghât, some of the gradients of which were one in six. The estimate for the timber was six lacs or three rupees a cubic foot delivered. The Anamallies at that time were delivering all their best timber at Poonani for the Bombay Dockyard, and for which they received Rupees 3-8 the cubic foot, so it was not worthwhile to sell under that sum to the Barracks delivered at Coimbatore; the cost of the carriage from Coimbatore to Wellington never was fairly known, as dozens of bullocks died in bringing up the timber, and were not charged to it. However, the case stood thus: the estimate for the timber was three rupees, and it was costing over Rupees 4-8 the cubic foot, and even at that price only a little was to be obtained. On arrival, I found the Ootacamund Timber Market had not a log over fifteen feet, and we required a very large number over twenty-four feet for girders. Fortunately, I was able to secure a rented forest, adjoining the Wynaad Teak Belt, and by 1860 or in less than four years, delivered two-hundred thousand cubic feet of timber to the Barracks at a cost of only one rupee the cubic foot, after all charges had been paid. In working this forest, I at once introduced elephants, the Coorumbers had to be trained to fell only the largest and best trees, as they were in the habit of felling a tree that would just measure about twelve cubic feet, as they were paid by the log. I introduced the system of payment by the cubic foot, and they soon learnt the value of it; at one time they gave much trouble, every large tree was "*Swami Tree,*" and could not be cut; even this difficulty was surmounted. Of course, on taking over a forest, worked by a native, it was necessary to re-organize the establishment, make roads, build carts, and in fact, provide for an extensive establishment. At

Saving by working a rented forest.

Reorganisation of establishment and new mode of working.

one time ten elephants and thirty carts were at work, as time compelled us to use our utmost exertions to get out as much wood as possible, not only to expedite the building of the Barracks, but to take advantage of the lease which expired in a certain time. Afterwards it was renewed for ninety-nine years, and some planting was begun; but I did not persevere in it as the lessee demanded a stump fee, and the land and climate being better further west in the Government Forest of Wynaad, I planted sixty acres there. The cost of carriage, some eight miles, was a charge, but then there was no stump fee, and the Teak grew straighter and faster further west. It would be still advisable in the west of Mudumalli Forest to put in germinated seed, as this would not be a plantation, and no stump fee would be payable. Amongst the public buildings supplied from these forests in addition to the Wellington Barracks were the Lawrence Asylum, all the bridges on the new Coonoor Ghât, Court-house of Ootacamund, Bangalore Barracks, numerous bridges in Wynaad. The surplus timber was sold by auction in Mysore and Ootacamund. I may here observe that in addition to all this emergent work, I was constantly at the Barracks superintending the work, and pushing it on. To expedite matters, I had twelve sets of sawyers, and thirty carpenters at work, at Gundulpett just outside the forest, they made up doors, windows and flooring, for two years they were employed, this in addition to a numerous staff at Wellington. I merely mention this to show the amount of work that had to be got through between 1856 and 1860, though I was not in the Forest Department at this time. I was obliged to do all the work of a Forest officer in addition to my engineering duties which were heavy. In 1860 having, by orders of Government, taken charge of the Forest Department, I had an opportunity of inspecting the various forests, and representing to Government their requirements.

Plantations. Stump fee.

Improve leased forest by seed sowing.

Public buildings supplied.

Anamallies.

After a visit to the Anamallies, in 1860, it struck me that sufficient attention had not been paid to the housing of the officers and their establishments. The situation of the buildings was in a hollow, and most depressing and unhealthy, the site was chosen because it was near the water ! ! and a better spot for catching fever could not well have been chosen. I selected a site on a ridge, a few miles off, close to the forest work, and where, by sinking wells, good water could be obtained. I further recommended that all the houses should be upstair ones; the sleeping rooms raised at least ten feet from the ground, as malaria rarely rises above that height. Several officers and overseers had lost their health mainly due to the position of the bungalows. Colonels Michael, Hamilton and Beddome, Messrs. Gosling and Douglas and many overseers. At Nellumbore it was the same, the bungalow was in a low place, though there was a hill some three hundred feet high a short distance off. I strongly recommended a good bungalow on the top. The difference of temperature alone in that sweltering climate must have been at least six or seven degrees, to say nothing of a healthy breeze. Too much importance cannot be attached to the situation of the forest residence, it should always have a sleeping apartment, at least ten feet aboveground. At Mudumalli, the hut was built on the rising ground, but it had no upper storey. It would be well if a proper bungalow, with substantial cooly lines, were built, as there is much planting to be done in this part of the forest. The Moplas in Malabar, as a rule, have upper stories to their houses, and no doubt they have a good reason for this style of building. All our forest houses should have upstair rooms, and we shall then have less of fever. With regard to the health of the establishment, I shall have something to say farther on.

Houses for forest establishment.

Major Campbell Walker has shown how floating is accomplished in his work, " Report on Forest management," possibly with some expenditure, for there is much blasting to be done, many of our hill streams could be utilised. At Goondry Wynaad, timber from the northern part of Wynaad is floated to Nungengode near Mysore. There are so many rocks in the Cubbany River that boats could

Floating Wynaad timber.

not work there. There are streams near Gooloor Hill in Beni, on the Survey Map, which lead into the "Nogo" river, from thence into the Cubbany River to Nungengode; these streams might be utilized for floating, especially if a large plantation of a thousand acres was made there. I planted sixty acres at Beni, and the growth of the trees was good. It is a fine site for a large plantation, the soil is good, the slopes are easy, the hills carry fine timber. Blackwood also grows well on them. As mostly all our timber had to be carted up to the Neilgherries for public works, it was not thought advisable to open up the floating capabilities of these streams, but as Madras offers such a good market for Teak, and the Mysore Railway is open, it is time to look to that city for a market. The same may be said of the Anamallies and Nellumbore. The floating on the Nellumbore river should be put a stop to. I wrote some eight years ago, recommending that a steamer, towing some four or five flat twenty-ton boats similar to those in use on the Buckingham Canal, should be used. The voyage from the furthest parts of the plantation to the Railway Station at Beypore would not take more than ten hours, and the boats could be towed back in the same time. The cost would certainly be less than the present charge which is about two annas a cubic foot. The present system is a most pernicious one. First bamboos which are scarce have to be cut and stored at a great expense of time, money and labor, and where labor is required for other work, the diverting of it, is at the expense of the plantations. Having collected the bamboos, they are made into a raft, on this the teak logs are placed, and a half flood chosen for floating—for if you float in a full flood, and your raft goes ashore, it must be taken to pieces as no power of elephants can push it off. Then the river, a narrow one, is blocked by numerous rafts, thefts of timber are common, the lashings are cut loose, the marks erased, and the owner vainly seeks the aid of the Police. The rafts frequently take three weeks to go to Beypore, sometimes they are left high and dry for months,

Floating Nellumbore.

in fact the confusion is endless. A steamer and a dozen twenty-ton boats would put a stop to all thefts.

The timber would be carried cheaply and expeditiously, the river would be always clear. If the steamer only worked for three months, carrying two hundred tons at a time or four thousand tons a month, the whole of the timber of those forests could be carried to Beypore with the greatest ease in two months. Moreover, there is, at times, a great scarcity of bamboos for floating timber. Teak, green, weighs over 60 lbs. the cubic foot and averages when dry 47 lbs. To leave it to dry in the forest, renders it liable to be stolen, as there are many private forests, and timber-stealing is very common. In 1874, when inspecting some new land, I had just bought for Government from the Amrapollium Rajah, I caught three elephants in the act of dragging some Teak across the river in open day. It is true, they did not expect me to appear in that particular part of the forest. The Rajah of Nellumbore complained that the Moplahs dived under his rafts, moored in front of his house, cut the lashings at nights, and floated the timber away. He was advised to use chains, and he did so, and lost no more timber at his depôt; but on the voyage down to Beypore, he had to pay Black Mail. So long as the Anamallies supplied timber to the Bombay Dockyard, it was floated to Ponani by river, but to send it to Beypore now, would be to compete with Nellumbore timber. For this reason it is preferable to send it to Madras where the consumption of Burma timber is very great, and the price high.

Steamer and Boats.

I am not aware that any of our forests require shoots or slips, the plan of a slip is laid down in "Reports on Forest management in Europe, by Colonel Campbell Walker." On visiting the Anamallies, in 1860, I was very much surprised to see what was called "a slip," it consisted of an inclined road about one in two, worn into large hollows. Elephants slipped the timber, when it lodged in the holes worn by rain—they had to lift it out again, thus the work instead of being simple and easy, was very laborious and expensive.

Shoots, slips.

The slip is no longer used, as a road at an easy gradient has been made, and the carting is done at one-half the cost of the slipping.

I observe that in my Forest Report for 1872, at page 62, I calculate the cost of slipping at 1-3 the cubic foot. I am certain the carting can be done for about one-half. Some

Seasoning Teak.

years ago a number of trees on the Anamallies were girdled with the view of seasoning them standing, as was done in the Burma Forests, it was not found to answer for when felled, the wood was found to be brittle, to have lost all its oil, and the axemen could not get a plank out of a log, of course, the system of girdling was abandoned. In 1862 the Admiralty sent out to India to enquire why Burma timber was so dry and brittle, whilst Malabar timber was full of oil and very tough. The papers were sent to me asking if the trees had not been tapped for oil, and I answered them to the following effect: "That Malabar timber was always left on the ground to season, lying in a horizontal position, so that all the sap and moisture was evaporated out of the log, whilst the oil remained, that the Burma timber was girdled and left standing for two years, that in consequence of this vertical position of the log, not only was all the sap drained away, but through the tubes all the oil was also drained away. That there was no reason why Burma Teak should not have as much oil as Malabar Teak if treated in a similar manner."

Girdling.

The advocates of girdling in Burma stated, "That as the timber had to be floated, it was necessary to leave it girdled for two years to reduce its weight. That if the timber were felled and left lying on the ground, it would infallibly be burnt as the area of the forest are so great that they could not afford watchmen to look after the felled timber." They did not seem to be aware that their system reduced the value of the timber by 50 per cent. I am of opinion that it would have been better to have formed large depôts and watched them, or to have put the timber on board flats and have towed them to the port.

As for rafting, it may do in some places like the Rhine where there is only a down traffic and a very broad river; but in many rivers, rafts interfere with the traffic, and it is a question, if there is not a saving in putting the timber on board flats and tugging them to their destination. One thing is certain that Burma timber is dry and brittle, and by no means so strong as Malabar, and the cause is the loss of oil. Floating.

In condemning rafting on certain rivers such as Nellumbore, I do not for a moment deny its utility on small streams, and on the Cubbany, and possibly other rivers where steamers cannot ply, in fact Wynaad timber cannot be got out to Mysore without floating, except by very expensive carting. In rafting it is advisable not to square the timber but to leave it round.

Habits of the Teak Tree.—It has been stated that "perfect drainage and a dry sub-soil" are absolutely necessary for the health of the Teak tree, page 356, Brandis' and Stewart's "Forest Flora;" now I have found that the Teak delights in a moist clayey sub-soil. All over Wynaad, Anamallies, Nellumbore, it will be found that the Teak grows best in a brown surface soil, having yellow clay as a sub-soil, the powerful roots of the Teak soon procure drainage for itself. If by perfect drainage is meant that Teak will not grow well in swampy situations, then the remark is correct; but I cannot agree, as to the preference of Teak for granite soils, in fact, nearly the whole of our sub-soils consist of decomposed felspar which are decidedly clayey in their nature. It is true, that at Nellumbore, the largest trees are seen on the banks of streams whose sub-soil is very free, but even then the clay predominates over sand, and the tree rejoices in a loose soil with plenty of moisture in it. Here we never find the Teak associated with bamboo, in fact, it is well known that Teak will not grow under bamboo. Wherever Teak is found in bamboo, it will at once be apparent that the Teak is older than the bamboo; Teak is found at the sea-level like Nellumbore, on the Anamallies 2,500 W., and in Wynaad up to three thousand feet growing well. Teak may be found on light and sandy soils, certainly not in Southern India. Teak does not live on humus, but on clayey sub-soils. I have shown that it is not "fire and early rains" that prevent seed from germinating, but rats and squirrels. A clean cut does not injure the tap root, page 358, Brandis' and Stewart's Flora. A forest cannot be called "small" that produces Teak trees of fifty to seventy cubic feet of timber, such as forty square miles in Wynaad, and over eighty square miles on the Anamallies. The question of "annual rings" was settled long ago. I have explained that the pith is not the cause of heartshake, but that the first made heartwood being not only softer than that made afterwards, but being older is the first to decay, for instance, when the rings are counted, it is found that the first rings are much further apart than the last—the first twelve rings will occupy a space of over an inch, the next perhaps only three-quarters, and so on, until the rings, at one hundred years, almost run into each other. Another curious fact is that the rings on one side of a tree will be wider than those on the other; this is due, I believe to the prevailing wind, the exposed side showing slow growth.

Article, Teak.—Again, it is stated that "quick grown Teak" is not the best, I agree with Lindley that fast grown timber is best. In a tree, thirty years old, there is no pith, it runs out at six feet from the ground.

Pith. I have examined trees seventy years old, and found no pith and no heartshake. I attribute the freedom from heartshake to the trees having escaped fire when young and being in their prime.

White ants. Much has been said about Teak resisting white ants, it does so as long as the oil remains in it, but should lime have extracted the oil when built in, it is no longer free from attack.

The Carpenter Bee or "*Xylocopa*" attacks Burma Teak which has no oil. I never knew it attack Malabar Teak though it bores through the hardest woods, such as Sāl, Hardwickia, binata, Jamboolanum, &c., &c. To prove if Teak has oil in it, the carpenter simply inserts his chisel, and by the faint appearance of oiliness on the tool, ascertains the fact.

Ship-builders complain of the quality of the timber they get from Pegu. Whether the trees stand an extra year after killing, or whether they remain seasoning in a ship-building yard after being squared, for a year or two, the result will probably be much the same. **Girdling Teak.**

We must look beyond this to find out the real cause of the loss of certain valuable qualities in Teak complained of. **Loss of oil.**

When this circular came to me, in 1866, I pointed out that girdling was the real cause of Teak, being brittle and devoid of oil, for if the sap descends by the capillary tribes, so does the oil. That if a tree is felled and lies horizontally for years, the oil does not escape, but the sap is evaporated out. That girdling trees was tried on the Anamallies in 1858 and proved a failure as the tree would not split, and the axemen could make nothing of it. I am aware that in Burma, they girdle Teak, because if felled and left on the ground for two years, it would be liable to catch fire, and Teak does not float until it has been seasoned at least two years—hence the reason of girdling—but nevertheless it ruins the timber.

It has been a well known fact for fifty years and more that Malabar Teak is superior to Burma, the chief reason being that Malabar Teak had retained its oil, whereas Burma Teak had lost it. It was supposed at one time that Burma Teak trees were tapped for oil. That Malabar Teak is not better than Burmese in other respects, for probably Atteran Teak grown in Burma is equal to any Teak if ungirdled.

CHAPTER III.

SANDALWOOD.

The Sandalwood tree is scientifically recognized as the *Santalum Album* or white Sandalwood belonging to the natural order *Santalaceæ* or Sandalwood family, a dicotyledonous plant composed of trees, shrubs and herbs,—the genus *Santalum* is the type, a small tree twenty or thirty feet with numerous branches forming more or less spherical heads, leaves opposite, on short stalks, oblong, smooth, entire, with a fine bloom below, panicles with their principal breadth in the middle axillary flower stalks opposite, usually three-flowered, with numerous, small, straw-colored flowers, changing to a deep purple, inodourous, the outer floral envelope or calyx four cleft, there being no inner envelope or corolla. Berry, round, smooth, and black, when ripe, succulent with a persistent calyx—the fruit is a celled nut solitary. The species are natives of Asia, the tropical parts of Australia, and the Pacific Ocean. The white Sandalwood is a native of Malabar on the hills of which it grows as a large tree. It is also found in Coimbatore, Mysore, Canara, Salem, Madras, &c. Mysore produces the best Sandalwood, two kinds of the wood are procurable in the market both being the produce of the same tree. The white Sandalwood comprises the outer layers of wood, is hard, heavy and susceptible of a good polish. The yellow or brownish wood is obtained from the heart of the tree, and is the most valuable and best esteemed. The heart or heavier wood comes chiefly from the lower parts of the stem, is strongly scented, hard, takes a good polish, and is well adapted for carving, turning, &c., and is easily cleft. The odour is strong and enduring due to the presence of an essential oil. The scent is dependent chiefly on the soil, and the elevation at which it grows a third kind of Sandalwood or Saunder's wood, or red Sandalwood as it is called, is met with in the market, the produce of the *Pterocarpus Santalinus* belonging to the natural order *Leguminosæ*, and produces a valuable dye, and takes a fine polish. Sandalwood is in great demand by cabinet-makers and other artizans more especially from China and India, it is largely used for carving ornaments, toys, fans, walking-sticks and for other ornamental purposes, also for burning the dead. A perfume obtained from the wood is in universal use in India and China. Its medicinal virtues are trifling, it has a bitterish, aromatic taste, and a degree of pungency which is not unpleasant. Its powder is believed to possess sedative and refrigerant properties, a mixture formed of cocoanut water is used to allay thirst, and is prescribed in fevers, headache and bilious affections; externally it is used as a cure for prickly heat by Europeans and to cool the system, as an incense, it is in general use especially by Mahomedans, and is burnt to perfume temples and dwelling houses both in China and India. The "*joss sticks,*" so generally used more especially by Mahomedans, and designated by them as the "*Ood buttee,*" consists of the raspings worked into a paste with water and spread on slender bamboo slips, are in every day use as a perfume and to keep away noxious insects. The wood rasped on a rough sandstone with water, and the resulting paste is used for marking the forehead, it is greatly appreciated as a cosmetic by all creeds and castes of people. The wood is in great request for cremation purposes among high caste Hindoos on account of its fragrance, a valuable oil is distilled from the refuse chips and roots which is always in demand, and generally used as a perfume and to adulterate the attar of roses. The fragrance of the wood increases with the age of the plant. The wood is usually cut into billets of fifteen, twenty, or thirty inches in length, and is sold by weight; the chips, cuttings, and roots form an article of commerce. The Sandalwood tree is subject to heartshake, it is not fit to cut under twenty years of age, the older it grows the more valuable it becomes till maturity is obtained in about fifty years. The low caste natives are fond of chewing the bark with their betel, in consequence of its pungency and do not hesitate to strip the trees when they can, much to their injury and eventual destruction, so much so that active steps are necessary to put a stop to this pernicious practice.

The price varies much, all depends on the China demand, it varies from three to six annas a pound.

Sites. *Sandalwood Plantations.*—Before forming a plantation, it is absolutely necessary to ascertain if Sandalwood grows in the vicinity, if it makes good heartwood, and its general rate of growth. Sandalwood grows at an elevation of two thousand to four thousand feet, three thousand being the mean. Mysore undoubtedly produces the best wood. In selecting a site, the ground should not be too rich, or you may have rapid growth, and but little heartwood as sometimes may be seen on the banks of streams where the stem may be a foot in diameter and yet all white wood. A fair brown soil is the best for producing good growth, and heartwood full of oil. If water be obtainable close at hand, so much the better, as a watering the first year, gives the plants a good start, and enables them to stand the hot weather. We will suppose you intend to make a plantation of at least one hundred acres. Small plantations do not pay. You will

Nurseries. make your nursery beds near water, they should be composed of sand and vegetable mould and ashes to keep off ants, &c. The seeds may first be germinated in a heap and then planted in lines, four inches apart, and three inches

Pits. in the lines. The beds may have light pandals of brushwood to break the force of the sun. When the plants are six inches high, they should be lifted, the tap roots cut back to four inches, and then replaced in the beds six inches apart. When nine inches to a foot in height, put them out with a transplanter into eighteen-inch cube pits, shade and water

Fences. for the first year. If possible, the plantation should be fenced with a ditch, and thorns planted thus,  as spotted deer are very destructive to the young plants, so are village goats. As the value of the Sandalwood tree depends upon the number of sound and straight billets you can get out of a tree, you must be very careful to draw your trees up as

Pruning. straight as possible, cutting off all unnecessary side branches, when not more than one inch thick close to the stem, if the branches are thicker, they must be shortened to a foot from the stem, for if you cut them close into the stem, the chances are that you have introduced rot into the stem, and thus reduced the value of your wood by one-half, for the Sandal tree is very subject to heartshake. The causes are, the Sholagurs have a habit of cutting into the stem of the tree to see how much heartwood it shows, deer rubbing the bark and injuring the cambium, natives barking the trees for the sake of its hot flavour, using it for chewing with betel instead of lime. Causing heartshake.

If your trees have been well planted without the roots having been disturbed, the chances are they will not require watering the second year, frequently it will be found advisable to use nurses to shade your young Sandal trees, and draw them up, for the first year or two, peppers are good at first, then for four or five years, acacias, or ceara, after which the nurses may be coppiced. Any fast growing tree serves. There is another reason why sandal thrives with nurses, it is semi-parasitical being next in natural order to Loranths in its habit, and the roots seem to grow best on other roots. Like the Orobanche the seeds of which will not grow unless their roots can be attached to the roots of another plant. It is not altogether shade that the sandal delights in—of course, annuals are of no use, fast growing acacias, &c., are best. The tree is fit to cut from twenty-five to forty years of age. It is not well to let it grow too old, or you may only have a hollow centre, and but little heartwood. In some stony soils, like Segoor, the sandal attains a thickness of no more than four inches, and yet ten miles off on the slopes of the Neilgherries, very large trees are found. The small trees generally contain more oil, and are harder and denser than the large ones. The heartwood of the smaller trees is very dark in colour, sometimes approaching red, whilst that of the large trees is from a deep to a light yellow. Shade. Trees should be planted eight feet apart shaded by nurses. Sandal roots parasitical.

In felling Sandalwood it is usual to take up the trees by the roots, as though Sandalwood does spring up from the stumps, the second growth is inferior and it is cheaper to replant, care must be taken to keep the billets in sheds, Cutting and felling.

or they split up in the dry winds, and much damage is caused.

Natural Sandal.

The tree is generally found in clumps of evergreen bushes and hedges at an elevation of from two to four thousand feet above the sea. The climate is what may be called rather dry, rainfall from thirty to fifty inches. Birds are very fond of the fruit which is something like a small purple grape, with a hard seed about the size of a pea. The birds carry the seed to hedges and trees and having eaten the pulp, drop the kernel which readily springs up under the shade of bushes or hedges—this has given rise to the native idea that to gernminate seed, it required to be passed through a bird!

Fires are very destructive to young Sandal trees, indeed they rarely survive them. There is a strip of dry forest from Guzulhutti in the south, to near Hasinoor in the north, elevated about one thousand feet above the Mysore plain, measuring nearly one hundred square miles where hardly a Sandal tree is to be found. The cause is the want of clumps of evergreen bushes and perpetual fires. In this strip Sholigurs fire the jungle to find deers' horns, to pick up myrobolans, and for pasture, though this jungle is surrounded by jungles bearing Sandalwood, I have never seen but one clump of evergreen bushes in which were Sandal trees. The cattle also were insufficient to keep down the grass, so that fires were a certainty.

Extension of natural Sandal by reserves, and crow-bar planting.

The best plan of extending natural sandal jungles is first to fence them to keep off cattle and deer, a ditch three feet wide at top, six inches at bottom, the loose earth thrown up on the inside, on the top of this the Mysore thorn should be planted. A piece not less than four square miles should be enclosed, and a regular establishment kept up. In the first showers crow-bar holes should be made in the clumps of evergreen bushes, and from the nursery, germinated seeds should be taken and put out in the first showers in June. This mode being the best for increasing a natural forest of Sandalwood trees. The process of filling and closing the holes should be the same as for Teak. Within the area of four square miles it will be probably found that two or three hundred acres are suitable for a plantation, if so, advantage should be taken of the establishment to secure their services for a regular plantation. In forming the Vyloor plantation, I was careful to ascertain the capabilities of the soil for producing Sandalwood of a good quality. I felled a tree near a ravine, it weighed 84lbs. when clean, stem and roots, the rings showed it to be twenty-five years old, and the heartwood was of first-rate quality. This set at rest the quality of the soil. This tree would probably have reached the age of forty years before it began to decline. The profits of an acre of Sandalwood are so great, that it is well worth a large outlay. Creepers are very destructive to Sandal trees, they should always be cleared away as they bend the heads of the trees, distort the stems, and frequently strangle the trees. I give an approximate balance sheet of a plantation of one hundred acres. The only data I have to go upon is the cost of the Vyloor plantations from their commencement. The average price of Sandalwood for many years, and the average yield over twenty-five up to forty years. If we plant 8 × 8, we shall have about seven hundred trees to the acre. We quincunx with nurses which are cut out when the trees begin to approach each other. There are two reasons for planting 8 × 8—one is that it saves watering, a very heavy expense; the other is that nurses draw up the trees and cause a good straight stem to be the rule—it also saves pruning a most important matter. Cassia florida is a fast grower, and makes a good nurse. If rubber trees are used as nurses, then from the fifth to the twentieth year, we should have

Sandal plantations.

some return from them, probably five hundred rupees an acre.—

First year planted.	Rs.
20 acres clearing ground ...	20
1,500 pits	15
1,500 plants...	9
Half Sandal, Half Nurses.	
Planting	10
Shading	6
Watering	20
Supervision	5
Rs.	85
Then 85 × 20 = ...	1,700
2nd year watering Rs. 10 ...	200
Supplying failures Rs. 5 ...	100
Weeding, Rs. 5	100
Supervision, Rs. 5	100
Cost of 20 acres, 2 years ...	2,200
3rd year weeding	100
Supervision...	100
4th year weeding	100
Supervision	100
21 years' Supervision ...	2,100
Pruning and weeding ..	2,100
	6,800
Interest, 5 per cent. for 12 years on Rs. 6,800 ...	4,080
Rs.	10,880
Felling and cleaning 1,500 maunds at As. 2 ...	3,680
Do. at 40 years 2,000 As. 2.	2,400
Supervision and Weeding, 15 years at Rs. 200	3,000
Interest, 15 years at on 14,500	3,375
Rs.	12,455

	Rs.
Sale of 500 trees, at 3 maunds, each at 5 Rs. per maund	7,500
	20
	1,50,000
200 trees at 41 years, 5 maunds per tree, 1,000 maunds × 20 acres = at Rs. 5	1,00,000
	2,50,000
Deduct charges	23,255
	2,26,745
On one acre = 11,337 or 11,337 × 100 = 1,133,700 or 282 Rs. an acre a year for 40 years.	
Tree's cost 1-4-0 each.	

10,880
12,455

23,335 Charge.

Price of Sandal.

The above estimate is, I think, well within the mark. The actual cost at Vyloor, for each tree at the end of eight years was 4 annas each. My balance-sheet shows the cost at twelve years, to be about 12 annas each, and at forty years, 1-8-0 each. Three maunds at twenty-five years is not in excessive yield—according to this estimate, the acre for forty years yields 282 rupees a year, and Teak gives 250 rupees a year over sixty years. The price of sandal depends much upon the China market; at one time it is as high as 9 rupees the maund of 25 lbs. for first class wood. Roots are bought for Sandalwood oil distilleries in South Canara where firewood is cheap. Roots at one time were only 2-8-0 the maund, but afterwards they rose to 4-8 the maund—so that 3 rupees the maund over all may be considered a fair average price. I have, many years ago shown, that if we had twenty years ago taken to planting Sandalwood largely, we should now be on the eve of reaping a very large crop, as it is, the department has to wait another ten years at least before any results can be arrived at.

Planting operations.

I may here remark that at Tulli Mulli where the Sandal plantations are, it would be easy to select, a good block of forest, four square miles at Vyloor the same. At Denkinicotta, in Salem, the same and various other places—but the Mysore plateau, ranging from two to four thousand feet, is undoubtedly the very best site for Sandalwood, and any departure from the conditions, as above laid down, would probably result in failure, for instance, to attempt to grow the tree in Malabar might be a success so far as the growth of the tree is concerned, but the scented oil would be deficient still it should be tried, and as the Conservator in Malabar has an experimental garden, it would be well if a few trees were tried there, but judging from what I have seen of Sandal trees growing near Vyloor on deep rich soil on the banks of streams, being nearly a foot in diameter and having no heartwood, though fully twenty years old, I fear it would be a failure, but here we require the chemist to tell us what forms the oil and heartwood, as the sap wood has no oil; the same may be said of Cinchona, what forms the alkaloids especially Quinine. A chemist for the departments is more urgently required than a botanist. One thing is almost certain, that trees require minerals to develop their special qualities more than humus or nitrogen; possibly lime, potash, and phosphoric acid are the three main ingredients. It is a curious fact that in Wynaad, though there is no free lime in the soil, yet both

Reserve blocks Sandal.

Sandal in Wynaad.

Minerals for trees.

Free Lime.

Teak and Blackwood, if wounded near the ground, contrive to absorb large quantities of lime, it may be seen encrusting the tree on the surface as far as four feet in height and six inches wide—so hard is the lime that it destroys circular saws, and the Curumburs use it for chewing with betel. Here we have an instance of a tree eliminating from the soil, a mineral that is not visible, and one that only exists incorporated, with another substance, such as Hornblend. The laboratory of nature is a very subtle process. It is probable that the Ceara Rubber Manihot Glaziovii will be found an excellent nurse for Sandalwood trees. I have found Sandalwood grow well near trees of the Ficus tribe, elastica especially, and the experiment is well worth trying. It would, of course, be necessary to train the rubber tree, so that it did not overshadow the sandal, as there are few trees that grow under the shadow of others; in fact, forty-nine out of fifty kinds of trees require shelter not absolute shade only partial. There is a further advantage in using the ficus tribe as they readily grow from cuttings. Ficus elastica could easily be procured; probably at the end of twenty years, it would be found advisable to cut out the rubber trees after having taken rubber from them for ten years.

There is another point, in using the Ficus or Euphorbiaceous tribe such as Siphonia elastica for nurses, they take and require but little moisture from the earth, nearly all they require is absorbed from the air.

CHAPTER IV.

ON DRY FORESTS.

Shutting up portions of forest.

FORESTS of this nature such as those on the Nullamullies in Kurnool, Salem, South Arcot, &c., should be treated as I recommended some years ago, *viz.*, a portion to be rigorously shut up for a period of at least ten years. No man or head of cattle allowed within the enclosed area which may be one hundred or a thousand acres. In dry forests it will be found that banks of streams are best for enclosures, there the soil is best and local moisture the greatest. To increase reproduction, the same plan should be followed as laid down for Teak, *viz.*, crow-bar pits and germinated seed wherever, practicable. I have impressed upon the Forester the absolute necessity of germinated seed, the sowing broadcast except under very favorable conditions is nine times out of ten a failure. It will, of course, be advisable to select the most valuable kinds for reproduction, such as certain Terminalias, *viz.*, Glabra, Coriaria, Hardwickia, binata, Soymida's febrifuga, Acacias—there is a long list to choose from, and only those should be selected that appear to thrive in semi-dry forests. It would be useless to plant Teak in the Cuddapah Hills, because trees found there are stunted; very frequently, it will be found in a semi-dry forest that whilst Teak is stunted, Vengay and Kura Murra thrive. In some of the Salem Hills, red cedar flourishes in the ravines at some elevation.

Increase of dry forest.

Best kind of trees.

In the north Sal is found in enormous quantities, on the Ballyrungums, the Michellia grows to great dimensions, Mesua and Hopea in our Canarese forests, also in Tinnevelly, see Beddome's Report, 18th August 1867, Appendix, Forest Report, 1867-68, No. 105, 20th April 1878, Beddome on Nellumbore.

Red cedar, &c.

CHAPTER V.

GENERAL REMARKS.

In the Forest Report (mine), 1871-72, Board of Revenue Remark, 5th August 1871, No. 3284, that "fires do not harm quite the contrary," on this I wrote, "of course, fires have their advantages, they render the jungle less pestiferous, and the young grass comes up earlier, but fires ruin saplings and should never be allowed in a reserved forest, but the difficulty is to prevent them. Formerly before the Forest Department was organized, there were three special causes which threatened to ruin all forests, *viz.*, the pernicious practice indulged in by the people of cutting saplings instead

Forest fires, cattle damage done by them.

of full grown trees which, though stopped; fires and cattle, remain to desolate the forests."

Plantations.

Forest Report, 1871-72, page 7, I wrote, para. 34: "These "consist of fine railway fuel plantations and one of the "valuable wood, red sanders. The fuel plantations gene-"rally are doing fairly. In the first three or four years the "work of establishing plants in so dry a district, is very "difficult and expensive; but though the plantation may "never pay by the sale of its fuel, still the surrounding "country will benefit as trees surely beget moisture."

"The Forest Department will thus indirectly benefit the "ryot. The formation of plantations has become a very "heavy item in forest expenditure, but were the whole "forest revenue expended in plantations and conservation, "Government would, in the course of years, be a large gainer. "What has already happened in Algeria threatens to occur "here, unless speedy measures are taken to secure reserves, "and save what yet remains of existing forests. Fires and "cattle are worse even than ryots, and should be excluded, "perhaps when Collectors are Conservators, they will be able "to use their authority to more effect than the Forest De-"partment has been able to do. I quite agree with the "Revenue Department that there is enough for all, if it is pro-"perly conserved, but that is the difficulty. In vain does the "Forest Department try to save the ryots from themselves, "their improvident habits too surely destroy the jungles "which ought to last them for centuries." On the subject of indiscriminate felling, the Collector of Coimbatore remarked

Ryots confined to their Village Jungles.

that ryots should be restricted to felling in their own village boundaries. I fully endorsed this view, and brought to the notice of Government that in Mysore wherever villages were

Hedge row timber.

distant from the forest, they cultivated hedge row timber in the shape of Neem Melia, Azedarach, Babool, A. Arabica, &c., &c. It surely is no hardship that if a village has destroyed its own small forest, it should be made to renew it and not indent upon forest that belongs to the country, and to which they can have no possible claim. It is the same with grazing rights, the reckless system pursued by ryots of depending chiefly on Government forests for their grazing instead of on their own exertions, and economizing their grass and fodder of various kinds. What was the case in England two hundred years ago? where cattle were slaughtered and salted, because they would not feed them through the winter, so the ryot in the dry season sends his half-starved cattle into the public forests to destroy them at his own sweet will, totally regardless of the mischief he is doing not only to himself, but to the public at large, in creating a decreased rainfall and scarcity of timber and fuel. Surely, as I wrote before, the ryot should be saved from his own destructive habits and taught that to destroy forests is not the way to benefit himself, and that by a little timely forethought, he might procure forage for his cattle without having recourse to the reckless system pursued by him for ages. The reckless destruction of his village jungle deprives him of firewood, this leads to his burning cattle manure for fuel. The field deteriorates in consequence, the crops are scanty, and the ryot impoverished. By taking some trouble, he could easily grow hedge row timber—this would supply building material and fuel, and thus lease the manure for the fields. Alas, the ryot, ground down for years by the Revenue officers, cares not to improve his opportunities, and prefers a life of careless ease? to one of forethought and labour. All these circumstances combined act and react one on the other, until it culminates in an impoverished peasantry, ever ready to succumb on the first season of scarcity. If we would improve the condition of the ryot, it is absolutely necessary to commence from the very foundation. It is not of the slightest use attempting to raise the status of the ryot, so long as we leave the main points of his position untouched; and until he is educated up to a certain point, he is quite incapable of appreciating any efforts made in his favour. It may be urged that this has nothing to do with forestry. I maintain it has, for we have to consider communal rights and to teach the ryot not to encroach

Grazing rights.

Burning cattle manure for fuel damage caused.

Education of ryot.

on reserved Government forests, and unless we can persuade him to adopt a new system of feeding his cattle, and supplying his fuel and building requirements, he will ever look fondly to those forests for supplying his wants without trouble or expense. It is to be borne in mind that the ryot has been for ages brought up under a reckless system of mismanagement, and new habits are not learnt in a day especially by a people who are the most conservative that the world has seen. From sire to son for ages, the same habits, trades, occupations have been the hard and fast rule.

Cultivation of Palmyra.

It would be well if the ryot, in some of the drier and poorer districts, were to cultivate the Palmyra more carefully—the leaves would do for thatching buildings, the stems for rafters, and the tree for sugar. Millions of trees might be grown in places which at present produce next to nothing. But the eternal laziness of the ryot prevents him from ever attempting to work for his descendants. There is an exception to this rule in Malabar where, on the birth of a daughter, a small plantation of cutch (Caesalpinia Sappan) is planted for her marriage portion.

Planting of Sappan in Malabar.

CHAPTER VI.

ACACIA MELANOXYLON.

Introduced by Colonel Dun.

THIS tree was, I believe, introduced by Colonel Dun to these hills about the same time as A. Dealbata, there were a few in 1845 in his compounds and some in the club grounds. They were still so rare in 1851, that I remember some just planted were stolen from General Watson's ground and were traced to a private gardener where they had been brought as a peace-offering, and up to 1857 the Government charged four annas for a plant. Last year I cut down a tree in my ground that had been planted before 1845 or about thirty-eight years of age. Though it had a large hole in it from which a hive of bees had been cut out, it gave sufficient planks to board a large room 24×15 of excellent wood, indeed so much is this wood esteemed in Australia that furniture is largely made from it. Here, I regret to say it is mostly used for firewood, it does not burn green like A. Dealbata nor does it produce so much tar, but is yet an excellent firewood. As far as I have observed the tree seems to flower and seed all the year round. The flowers are inconspicuous, but the seed pods seem at times to cover the tree. It is a very valuable tree, and should be cultivated more largely. It does not grow as fast as the Eucalyptus nor is it so tall, but some trees that are forty years old contain at least fifty cubic feet of good timber, as a rule, it makes black heartwood in a similar manner to our Dalbergia Latifolia. Its uses.

CHAPTER VII.

OUR DEPÔTS.

MANY years ago I advocated great central Depôts of Teak and other wood. First at Madras where the consumption of Teak is very great. There should be an officer in charge; he could indent upon the various forests for a supply for his timber yard. It seems a great farce that Government should be compelled to go into the market to purchase timber of merchants at a considerably enhanced rate, when it could be supplied at a fair rate from the Government forests—at every head-quarters there should be a Depôt; at Trichinopoly the officer should indent upon the Anamallies or Beypore for his timber. By having Depôts, Public Work officers, instead of employing contractors, would simply have to draw their timber from the Depôts selecting such scantlings as suited them. The Gun Carriage sometimes sent an Agent to the Anamallies for Teak and Blackwood, this gave rise to endless complaints, logs were changed *en route* to Madras, and the blame could never be fairly laid on the right party. When Vengay was selling in Madura at 1-8-0 the cubic foot, Teak was bringing but one rupee at Calicut. At Palghat, merchants ask now 2-12-0 the cubic foot—while at Calicut, timber (Teak) is sold by Government for 1-8-0, and at Ootacamund for two rupees the cubic foot. The officers of divisions should have full control over their timber yards, and indent when necessary upon other timber yards for a supply of any particular timber for which there was a demand.

CHAPTER VIII.

LABOR.

In Wynaad the axemen are Corumbers, and very good workmen. They also are very useful for Teak plantations, many are intelligent, and the great advantage of employing them is that they live in the forest all the year round, they fell and square timber with great precision, they can also be trusted in planting out operations; for cartmen, road labor, &c., Canarese are employed. Sawyers are obtained from Mysore and other parts. On the Anamallies, men from Palghaut are employed as axemen, they were very expert in dividing by means of wedges very large trees into planks suitable for dockyard purposes. The Kadirs, a jungle tribe, are useful for building huts, the Mahouts there and in Wynaad are generally Musselmen, whereas at Nellumbore and those parts, they are almost invariably Punniars, and as the Nellumbore elephants are used without harness, dragging by their teeth, the equipment of a Punniar and his elephant may be said to amount to *nil*. These Punniars obtain an extraordinary influence over their elephants, and especially the males by a peculiar process. The local labor at Nellumbore is made up of Malayalums and some Moplahs, there are many trained men amongst them who understand planting and pruning.

CHAPTER IX.

HEALTH OF ESTABLISHMENT.

This most important point deserves careful consideration, for on it depends whether your forest can be worked or not to advantage and profit. Where there is a fixed staff employed permanently, they should all be *compelled* to sleep in rooms at least ten feet above the ground, the lower rooms might be converted into stores, offices, cattle sheds, &c. The water should be drawn from a well, if possible, and should be tested occasionally with per maganate of potash to ascertain if it is free from impurities, one grain is sufficient for this purpose—if pure, the water shows a lovely pink deepening to violet with a larger dose, but turning to brown if the water is unfit for use for drinking and cooking purposes. Jungle-fever invariably breaks out on the thirteenth day counting from the first night of sleeping in the jungle, and if precautions are taken within the thirteenth day, such as an aperient dose followed up by five grains of quinine a day or two previous to the thirteenth day, the fever, if not averted, will be very much modified. Sleeping in musquito curtains will be found an excellent safe-guard. Natives invariably cover their faces with their cloths when sleeping which acts in the same manner, *viz.*, by preventing the entrance of malarious gases—on the same principle as the safety lamp of Sir Humphrey Davy. The Italian Doctors have lately discovered that in the blood of the fever patient, there are numbers of infusoriæ which were destroyed by the taking of quinine. It is of little use taking quinine until the bowels have been cleared out, nor should it be administered on an empty stomach. The mixture for fever in Ceylon was a table-spoonful of salts, a tea-spoonful of jalap and half a tea-spoonful of quinine, all mixed together in a wine-glassful of water. Natives delight in emetics, and no doubt in the early stages of fever they are very useful, five grains of Ipecacuanha, with one-and-half grains of tartar emetic in a pint of water taken, in three or more doses according to the action, within an hour (as no two people bear the same dose) followed by lots of hot water when vomiting has begun. I have sometimes had as many as twenty bandymen in a row taking emetics, and all my work stopped. Sometimes a wave of fever passes over a forest and prostrates nearly every man even Corumbers, sometimes not escaping. A large stock of Cinchona Alkaloids should always be kept in the forests; for dysentery, ten to fifteen drops of laudanum in a table-spoonful of castor oil, and constant doses of three to four grains of Ipecacuanha will, in some cases, give great relief. Chlorodyne also is much liked by natives, a gall-nut called by the natives "Mashikkay," *Quercus infectoria* or Galls, and common in the bazaars, one nut ground down, will afford three doses. Phenyle for cuts and bruises and ulcers that follow any hurt after fever, will be found very valuable, mixed either with water as a wash or cocoanut oil in the proportion of one part to 50—as an ointment laid on a rag—is excellent for man and beast, a small portion of bees wax should be melted with cocoanut oil to give it consistency. Phenyle is also useful for the bites of ticks, leeches, musquitoes, scorpions, and used pure would be useful instead of caustic in dog or snake bites when nothing else is available. I have been thus diffuse on this subject, as medical advice is not to be had in forests, and I have always had to depend on my own resources. On one occasion I arrived in the forests to find my people on the eve of a stampede, two or three people just come from Mysore had been seized with cholera and died. By a judicious admixture of cholera pills and advice, I restored confidence, and work was resumed; had I not opportunely come to the rescue, work, at a most important time, would have come to a stand still for a month. In camping out, natives are very fond of banks of streams because water is handy, totally ignoring the fact that these are the most deadly spots, especially if bamboos are growing there; always choose a ridge if possible over which the wind blows freely, live well, never get up before sun-rise or stay out of doors after sun-set, keeping all doors closed. Never drink jungle water, weak tea with lime juice without milk or sugar, will be found excellent for working upon. My diet in the forests, during the middle of the day when I have frequently walked upwards of thirty miles, was a couple of hard boiled eggs, a large chupatti, made of coarse flour, and for drink, a bottle of weak tea, which lasted me from sun-rise to sun-set. I never drank jungle water, if very thirsty, in the pursuit of elephants in the hot weather, I chewed the fruit of the

Nellekai" (Emblica Officinalis), a fruit which looks like a large green gooseberry in clusters on the trees. Astringent at first, it causes a flow of saliva and sweetish taste. One hot morning, in April, I was informed that a large herd of elephants had beset the cartmen and interrupted their work; everything was at a dead lock, so to stop this state of affairs, I sallied forth at sun-rise, and an hour or two walking, brought me into the centre of the herd, numbering some sixty or seventy; by one o'clock I had run the herd to a standstill, and had slain three tuskers, the ground underfoot consisted of ashes, as the grass had been just burnt, the swallowing of these fine ashes, added to the heat of the weather, and the exertions requisite to follow the herd, were such as to create a thirst of no common kind, and yet on a bottle of tea, and two or three "Nellekais," I walked back to camp, feeling none the worse for my exertions. I have often, on the hills, in a blazing sun, in January, tried the effects of cold water from a purling stream, the more I drank, the more I desired to drink, and no amount seemed capable of quenching one's thirst; indeed I may say that weak tea, with lime juice (if it is warm so much the better), is the only drink capable of assuaging a raging thirst.

CHAPTER X.

TREATMENT OF SEEDS.

SEEDS require very various treatment. Casuarina and Cinchona being very light, hardly require to be covered at all; others, such as Teak and Sandalwood may be buried to the depth of at least half an inch with advantage; in sending seeds to a distance especially those which quickly lose their vitality, such as mahogany, it is advisable to pack them in damp earth, so that they may go on germinating in transit. Tea seeds from China were brought over in this way in a Wardian case by Captain Mann, and on arrival, were found to be germinating by thousands. The late failure of mahogany seed sent to the Agricultural Gardens at Madras where 90 per cent. of the seed failed, would not have occurred had they been treated in the abovementioned manner, it may be safely said 90 per cent. would have germinated, and a most valuable tree introduced by thousands into this country. The small expense of a Wardian case would have been as nothing in comparison with the importance of the success of the experiment, even in sending valuable seeds from one part of India to another, it is well to ensure success by putting them into damp earth; seeds should never be packed in *tin* because the extra moisture cannot escape, and may rot the seeds if they are very many days in transit. This is found especially the case when seeds are packed damp in hermetically sealed tins. On one occasion, a gentleman sent me (what I learnt afterwards had been some favorite bulbs from his garden) in a tightly soldered tin case, but which appeared to be on opening a dish of cooked onions. Seedsmen at Home appear to be exceedingly ignorant as to the packing of seeds, and pack them imperfectly dried in this pernicious manner, and then are surprised to find they had turned out a failure. There are many ways of sending cuttings of valuable plants. I give the palm again to the Wardian case, more especially so, for the packing of succulent plants ; but for cuttings of all but soft wooded plants, the ends may be tied up in damp moss, or dipped in bees-wax (melted) and rolled up in wax-cloth and sent by Parcel Post or Banghy. Glass houses are chiefly useful by enabling you to regulate the temperature either in hot or cold climates—in the former, glass and shutters would be necessary. One principal rule must always be kept in mind, and that is, that for all cuttings the bottom heat must be greater than that above, say 90° below, 80° above; another is perfect ventilation; the 3rd to have alternate strips of blue and white glass, the blue color exercising a most important effect on vegetation, the growth being twice as fast under that color. In 1860 when I was entrusted with the direction of the Cinchona experiment with Mr. McIvor as my Executive, it was of the very greatest importance to ascertain how Cinchona could be best propagated? Numerous experiments were instituted in the treatment of both seeds and cuttings, and it was found that a glass house was indispensable, and I may say that the success of the experiment would have been jeopardized had the advice of certain incompetent persons been adopted. *See* Cinchona Blue Book.

Fortunately better counsels prevailed, and I had the satisfaction of seeing my ideas carried out. It was also found that after a few experiments, the propagation of the plant by seeds and cuttings was by no means difficult, where first principles were carried out, and correct appliances used.

Between 1861 and 1865 Mrs. Morgan alone turned out upwards of half a million of plants from cuttings. From fifty seeds of Cinchona Condeminea no less than twenty-five thousand cuttings were made from the fifty plants, the seed produced within two years.

Just now, 1883, it is very important to raise plants from cuttings of the more valuable kinds of India rubber producing trees. If a certain strain of plant is to be kept up, cuttings must be resorted to; seed is never safe especially Cinchona seed. I am not aware if cuttings of mahogany have been tried as it is a leguminous tree, they would probably succeed. It is very necessary to have some idea of the soil you are going to plant, for instance, Teak will not grow in pure sand nor will Casuarina grow in clayey ground. The Larch prefers a sandy soil, the Oak, a clayey soil. In a country like India, it is essential to study Isothermal lines and not make the blunder of planting Pinus Maritima in the low country, as was done some years ago. It is true, that some trees have a wide range of habitat, but these are exceptional, and only prove the rule. It was considered that the higher Cinchona Succirubra was planted the greater would be the yield of Quinine; but there was a limit, for it was found that the west of Ootacamund the tree would not grow over six thousand feet, but east it grew well at that elevation. The same with Cinchona Calisaya, this would not

7

grow well at even five thousand feet west of Ootacamund, but at Coonoor, it grew well up to six thousand feet. The fact being, the west of Ootacamund in consequence of the hot air of the Wynaad plateau being tempered by an elevation of three thousand feet, and much forest, whereas at Coonoor, the hot air came up direct from a bare country, only one thousand feet above sea-level, thus six thousand feet at Coonoor was nearly as warm for vegetation as four thousand five hundred feet west of Ootacamund. So that in calculating heat due to elevation, some other matters have to be taken into consideration, *viz.*, rainfall, prevailing winds, height of low country above the sea, nature of the country, forest or otherwise, gorges, ravines, &c., through which the hot air ascends, and the cold air descends, thus equalising the temperature—whilst on the subject of the scientific treatment of plants, seeds, &c., it is much to be regretted that the services and knowledge of the Superintendent of the Ootacamund Gardens are not utilised for the teaching of Overseers, Foresters, and others. The Forest officer has not time to train men in this department, nor has he any appliances, whereas they may all be found in the Ootacamund gardens. The application of the Overseers' training may be practically carried out at Nellumbore and our other important forests. The great drawback in our forests is their unhealthiness, a trained man being frequently lost through fever which is no respector of persons.

CHAPTER XI.

LIST OF USEFUL TREES WITH REMARKS.

In this list besides timber trees, there is a great variety of trees that might be cultivated with advantage for their economic products.

No. 1 Teak, Tectona grandis. *Remarks.*—Grows at the sea-level and up to three thousand feet elevation, cannot be well grown except in moist situations; like the Oak, prefers a rather retentive sub-soil, though it grows well at Nellumbore in a sandy clay, but just as often in soft laterite, which has all the appearance of a stiff clay. Though in Wynaad there is no visible lime to be found in the soil; this tree has the singular property of absorbing lime from the soil which forms in the shape of long strips, encrusting the outside of the tree in lengths of three and four feet, and in width from three inches up to a foot, and two and three inches in thickness. The Curumbers use it instead of lime for betel chewing. Teak cannot be grown amongst bamboos, nor indeed can any other forest tree. It is a fallacy to suppose otherwise, and wherever the contrary has been observed, it is due to the fact that the trees were established there before the bamboos appeared, for though bamboos may grow amongst trees, young plants of trees are poisoned by the acid emanations from bamboos, the same is the case with the Tamarind tree under which even grass will not grow. The mode of growth of the Teak tree depends very much on its situation, such as at Nellumbore, for instance, where the climate is exceedingly forcing, the trees are drawn up to a very great height at forty years of age, being something like hundred feet high, after which age, their vertical growth is slow, and the boles begin to fill out. In Wynaad owing to the difference of climate, the growth is much slower, probably not quite two-thirds of the above rate. In the Anamallies the growth is between that of Nellumbore and Wynaad—and at the same time the trees attain a gigantic height. In testing timber at the Neilgherry Barracks, it was found that the long straight grain of the Anamallie timber deflected more than that of Wynaad, thus showing that the Wynaad timber of slower growth was more rigid and better adapted for girders—in fact, if all things are considered; very probably, Wynaad Teak is superior for building purposes to any other Teak timber. The carpenters at the Wellington Barracks always complained that the Wynaad timber was far more difficult to work up than that from Anamallie.

A great many complaints have been made that "Tukkul" or native clearings in the forest destroys the Teak; this Tukkul may be true when all the Teak trees have been cut over and burnt, but I have known instances where Teak trees having been left in the clearing, the ground, in a few years, afterwards was covered with Teak seedlings. I also remarked in one particular instance that in a "Tukkul" clearing, all the young Teak trees had been ruthlessly cut over by the Curumbers, but owing to the fire not having been a severe one, or the clearing having been abandoned before fire came in, every tree had thrown out a shoot, and when I saw it in 1860, it looked like a regular plantation, the cut in the bole could be distinctly traced, every tree was drawn up as straight as an arrow, and they appeared about thirty years old. The Teak has some enemies, for instance, I have already shewn how rats and squirrels destroy the seeds when planted in beds, sometimes mealy bug attacks the tap roots, and one year I lost twenty thousand plants from this cause—the cure is, plenty of ashes in the beds. Elephants sometimes destroy the trees by walking through a plantation. Sambur also by rubbing their horns against the young trees, do considerable damage, monkeys jumping from tree to tree, break the tops. Colonel Beddome, in his Forest Report for 1869-70, page 44, mentions a small area of superb Teak, nine feet in girth and sixty to seventy feet high. He states that the Teak has not spread, this only exemplifies what I have stated before that Teak does not spread, that in fact to even hold its own, it requires peculiar conditions. The Teak seems to have been found in the Golcondah Taluq of Vizagapatam, at an elevation of two thousand feet.

Black wood, Dalbergia Latifolia.

This tree attains a vast size on the Anamallies, Wynaad, and the slopes of the Neilgherries above Nellumbore, planks three feet in diameter are not uncommon, it is considered by the natives to be stronger than Teak, and is generally used in parts where a considerable strain is to be met, it is of slower growth than Teak, and has the same peculiarity of drawing up lime from the soil, especially where the bark has been injured. The demand for this wood in Bombay is very considerable, being in great requisition for the carved furniture for which that Presidency is famons, and for furniture of all kinds, it is generally found growing singly in the forest. I once saw a tree on the Anamallies which squared to six feet, it is a profitable wood to cultivate, the price varies from two to three rupees and eight annas a cubic foot.

This tree is gradually becoming scarce from the increased and enormous consumption of it in China the seeds are naturally sown in the jungle, being carried about by birds, and being enveloped in a fruity pulp, it is eagerly eaten by many birds. It is a very profitable tree to cultivate, and there are thousands of suitable acres available in the Suttiamungalum, Collegall, Denkinicotta and a few other Taluqs. Sandalwood, Santalum album.

This tree grown in the Cuddapah jungles is in great demand, the straight logs are used for posts, the crooked pieces are exported for dyeing purposes,—a profitable tree to grow, takes a beautiful ruby polish. Red Sanders, Pterocarpus Santalinus.

This wood is good building timber and makes very handsome doors. The grain is close and takes a high polish, grows in Teak forests and attains a very large size; it is also found growing well in dry forests. It is a valuable wood of fairly fast growth. Vengay, Pterocarpus Marsupium.

This tree is found in Sandalwood jungles, is valuable for furniture, but it does not arrive at any size in this country. The Ceylon tree produces logs of twenty cubic feet and makes valuable furniture and panelling wood; it takes a high polish, perhaps if grown in moister jungles in this country, it might attain a greater size. Satinwood, Chloroxylon Swietenia.

This tree found growing wild in Wynaad, and attaining a vast size, is valued for its building properties, also for furniture, the wood at first of a bright yellow color turns with age to mahogany. The fruit too is very valuable, and is too well known to require any description here. The seeds are not unlike chesnuts when roasted, and very nutritious. The Artocarpus incisa or Bread fruit should also be largely planted. Jack tree, Artocarpus integrifolius.

Achawood, Hardwickia binata.

This tree found principally in the Salem dry jungles, is remarkable for its hardness, turning the edge of the sharpest steel tools, for certain purposes where hardness, density, and strength are required, it is very valuable, its properties are but little known especially in Europe. Bunjarras destroy the young trees by thousands for the sake of their bark from which they spin a coarse rope;. this tree might be cultivated with advantage.

Hopea species?

A valuable wood for building purposes found principally in South Canara. *See* Beddome.

Red cedar, White cedar, Chickrassia tabularis, and Cedrela Toona.

Very valuable timber tree grows to a huge size in Wynaad—very light but durable, considerably used for furniture and building purposes.

White and Black Muttee, Terminalia arjuna and tomentosa.

The two Terminalias, white and black Muttee are very much esteemed by the natives for their timber. The white Terminalia grows on the banks of streams in the Salem, Coimbatore, and other dry forests. The black Muttee is found in vast numbers in Wynaad, Anamallies, Nulla Mullies, &c., it has a very straight growth, and is very strong.

Acrocarpus fradinifolia.

This gigantic tree found in Wynaad, is largely used for building purposes, it cuts up a bright pink, looks like red cedar.

Erool, Inga Xylocarpa.

Very hard dense wood found useful for railway sleepers.

Sal. Shorea robusta.

Very good timber, does not grow large in this Presidency except in the north.

Casuarina municata.

Said to have been introduced from the Sunderbunds,—hard, heavy, strong wood, useful for building. The above are our principal forest timbers. There are others, such as Acacia Speciosa, Oderatissima, Ebony, &c., &c., which are useful.

Mahogany, Swietenia Mahagoni.

Introduced Woods.—This most valuable wood for furniture, veneering, &c., grows well at Madras, and probably would grow even better at Nellumbore, unfortunately the tree does not seed readily. Those in the Agri-Horticultural Gardens, Madras, though some forty years old, have only given some two or three pods in their life. Introduced seed, by the way it was packed abroad, nearly all failed. It should have been packed in semi-dry earth, and thus would not have become dried up. Great efforts should be made to introduce this tree into our forests near the coast.

The Ceara promises to be a great success, it seems to grow from the sea-level up to three thousand feet; as a nurse for Sandalwood trees, it will probably be found invaluable,—trees have already been tapped in Ceylon with favorable results. **Rubber trees, Manihot Glaziovii, or, Ceara rubber.**

The introduction of this tree into our forests would be a great boon. In South America, it is food and drink; it is called there the Hya, Hya. Said to have been introduced into the Bombay Forests. **Milk or Cow tree, Galactodendron (Brosimum) utile.**

There are several very valuable kinds, one from Burmah is said to be very large. Planted along river banks, it is invaluable for preventing their erosion. **Bamboos, Bambusa arundinacea, nana, and gigantea.**

In our Hill Ranges, these trees grow well and are very useful for house building, &c. Varieties from Queensland may yet be found suitable for growing in the low country. **Eucalyptus Globulus.**

This grows well from three to six thousand feet elevation; it is said to produce wood suitable for cask staves. **Grevillia Robusta.**

This valuable wood would certainly grow well in a climate like that of Nellumbore. **Camphor tree, Camphora officinarum.**

The same remark applies to this tree. **Gutta-percha, Isonandra gutta.**

In Florida this timber is exported largely to England, it is also valuable for its pitch producing qualities, would grow well on most of our hills. **Pinus Rigida, Pitch Pine.**

Grows well at Madras and Bangalore. I have seen some trees whose heads were fifty feet in diameter and loaded with pods. The tannic acid is valuable. **Divi Divi, Cæsalpinia Corriaria.**

From Australia, the percentage of tannin in the bark of this tree is very high, grows from four to seven thousand feet elevation. **Acacia Decurrens.**

A. Melonoxylon. This is the furniture wood of Australia, grows from five to seven thousand feet elevation,—a valuable tree.

A. Dealbata. Habitat the same as above; bark valuable for tanning, wood good for burning.

Cocoa, Theobroma cacao. This, though only a small tree, might be found useful for shading ground under Teak trees; does not grow well over fifteen hundred feet above the sea-level, might be planted when all but two hundred trees are cut out in the acre.

Bixa Orellana, Arnotto. The same remark applies to this bush. The pods are valuable for their dye, and Arnotto for coloring cheese is well known. The seeds give a fine flavor when ground up with cocoabeans. Grows up to three thousand feet elevation.

Iron wood, Mesua ferrea. A very useful, hard, heavy wood.

Ebony, Diospyros Melanoxylon. Grows best in the Travancore forests.

Poon. Sterculia fœtida. ? Splendid specimens on the Carcoor Ghât, first-rate spars of this tree are said to be worth one thousand rupees on the coast.

Notes on Eucalyptus Globulus.—This tree was planted at Ootacamund by General Fred. Cotton, then Captain Cotton, about the year 1843, there was one in the ornamental sholah at Gaton then his property, and there were three trees in his garden at Woodcote.

In 1852 Mrs. Morgan drew my attention to the seeds of a tree at Colonel Havelock's house, this was a species of Eucalyptus, we raised about four hundred plants from its seed, and finding the growth extremely rapid about ten feet a year, I was induced to obtain a quantity of Eucalyptus seed from Australia in 1856, and in a short time raised over one hundred and fifty thousand plants, and distributed them all over the hills. So rare were the plants that even in 1867 the Government Gardens priced a plant at twelve annas, and had the hills trusted to the gardens for the general cultivation of this wonderful tree, they might never have been planted to the extent they now are!! In 1862 Sir William Denison, the then Governor, seeing how successfully the trees grew, ordered some Government land to be planted, and this was the commencement of planting on a large scale.

The tree at Gaton far outstrips any other on these hills. At six feet from the ground it girths fourteen feet and has four hundred cubic feet of timber. There are trees in my garden "The Retreat" planted about 1857 averaging one hundred and forty feet in height and eight feet round, at three feet from the ground. They are, of course, specially fine trees grown on a loose bank of earth and much sheltered. There are twelve that contain one hundred and fifty cubic feet of timber up to one hundred feet from the ground leaving forty feet of top. Size of Eucalyptus.

I had a tree, cut down at Tudor Hall, about the year 1868, it was an average tree grown in good soil. Mr. Broughton, the Government Quinologist, and myself had it carefully weighed, the total weight of tree including top, roots, &c., was one thousand seven hundred and fifty pounds, of this sixty per cent. was moisture. The age of the tree was eight years. The growth of the Eucalyptus averages eight feet a year up to a certain age, which may be taken at about fifteen years. I have measured many trees about one hundred and forty feet in height at that age, after this age, the trees seem to increase in bulk, but not in height. The Eucalyptus has been credited with keeping off malaria in marshy places by the aromatic scent of its leaves; this is only partly correct, for the fact is that the tree having very powerful roots, pierces through the bed of clay that retains the moisture, and thus drains marshy lands, for the water descends to a lower level. I have, on these hills, seen small ponds and streams dried up where Eucalypti have been planted. In many parts of Italy where Pinus Maritima has been planted, the ground has been completely drained, and the malaria banished. At Arcachon, in France, there was a very considerable tract of land, full of marshes, with stunted Oak, Bech and Elm growing, the place was the resort of snipe and woodcock. The trees were cut down, and the whole planted with the turpentine yielding fir, the result was that the ground was com- Eucalyptus Globulus.

pletely drained, and the place become a sanitarium for invalids. In Algiers the planting of the Eucalyptus has, in numerous cases, banished malaria by simply draining the land.

The tree is of very great use here for ordinary building purposes, the thinnings at eight years of age makes excellent rafters and wall plates, nor do they easily decay if the bark is kept on and the wood protected. Planking from older trees lasts fairly well, if not exposed to damp, but this is no test as we have no timber so to speak; the oldest trees being only twenty-five years old, and nothing being considered timber under forty years. I may here observe that by steeping the planks in a tank of water which contains $\frac{1}{600}$ part of lime, the durability is much increased. There is no necessity for putting more than one cubic foot of lime to six hundred cubic feet of water, as no more lime can be taken up by the water—the theory is that the water forces out the sap and deposits lime in the capillary tubes.

Of the wood as timber.

Eucalyptus varieties.

In the year 1862 I obtained a large variety of Eucalyptus from Australia, none of the Jarrahs succeeded, it being too cold for them, but the red gum Eucalyptus rostrata has done well, it is reckoned a most valuable timber in Australia, it is nearly allied to Jarrahs; Eucalyptus Amygdalina also grows well—this tree is reported to exceed even the Wellingtonia Gigantea in height, trees of nearly five hundred feet in height having been measured. The grain of Eucalyptus Globulus is similar to that of the ash.

I may here remark that as a rule plantations 6 × 6 succeed best as the trees draw each other up, and fine straight stems are the result. Thinning out is best at eight years in average situations, of course, there are plantations in very rich soil that require thinning even at six years. Some years ago, Forest Report, 1861-62, I compared the growth of the Eucalyptus with Teak at Nellumbore and Oak plantations in England, and found that Teak grows twice as fast as Oak, and Eucalyptus twice as fast as Teak. I have already mentioned another example, there are some twenty-five trees planted in front of my present house, I know their age to be about twenty-five years, they are one hundred and forty feet in height, and average one hundred and twenty cubic feet each—this rate of growth is only half that of the single tree at Gayton but yet it is enormous, compared with Teak which, in good situations, does not average more than one cubic foot a year.

The tree grows best in what are called shola soils, that is where natural woods grew before, these are composed of humus to a depth of two or more feet with a sub-soil of decomposed felspar which remains moist throughout the year, next certain grass lands which have a peaty surface soil and a retentive sub-soil. So powerful are the roots of the Eucalyptus that they rapidly bore through a bed of clay, and thus drain any marshy place as has occurred in Algeria, indeed on these hills, they are accused of drying up springs. The fact being that their roots having bored through the substratum of clay that prevented the water descending to a greater depth, the spring has followed the roots to a lower level. Soils.

The tree Eucalyptus Globulus delights in an elevation of seven thousand feet, and bears ten degrees of frost; a rain fall of fifty inches a year suits it well. The mean temperature of Ootacamund is 56°. The tree does not, in this latitude, 12° north, succeed below five thousand feet elevation—it has been tried and failed. Cold and elevation, rain fall temperature.

The trees are usually laid out six feet by six feet, or say twelve hundred to the acre; at ten years of age, half are taken out to enable the rest to come on, the balance are gradually thinned out until only one hundred trees stand on the acre, as per balance sheet of a Eucalyptus plantation. Mode of planting.

The wood when ten years old is good for all kinds of rafters used in building; when twenty years old, it is fit for flooring planks, rafters, reepers, &c., when forty years old, it may be considered to be timber and has been used for ships, spars, &c.—it has a fine long grain something like ash. Oil has been distilled from the leaves, and used for rheumatism, and cigars have also been made from the leaves and smoked for bronchitis and asthma. The twigs which are shed being full of resinous matter are collected by the poor who have blessed the introduction of the tree, as with little trouble Uses of the wood.

and no expense, they can soon collect a bundle, and to poor natives coming up from the low country where the thermometer is ninety odd and never under sixty; cheap fuel is a great boon, the leaves being full of oil also burn well. There is another Eucalyptus; rostrata or red gum, this grows nearly as large as Eucalyptus Globulus, the wood is quite as good, and it furnishes a red gum highly astringent called gum kino and very useful in dysentery. Other varieties of Eucalyptus have been introduced here by me. Varieties of the Jarrah, one of the finest timbers in the world, but unfortunately it thrives in a warmer climate. Eucalyptus Amygdalina has also been grown, this tree is the wonder of the world. Some stems measured in Australia were nearly five hundred feet in length, exceeding the Californian Giants Wellingtonia Gigantea in height. Several species from Queensland Hill will no doubt be found to suit the climate of Mysore, and perhaps even the low country, but of this, I am doubtful. Eucalyptus Globulus would not even grow in Coorg.

Balance Sheet of an acre of Eucalyptus Globulus from 1 year up to 40 years:

Expenditure.	RS.	*Receipts.*	RS.
Clearing ground ...	10	Sale of 500 trees = 125 tons, at 8 Rupees a ton ...	1,000
Cost of plants, 1,200 ...	6		
Pits, 1,200, 18" cube ...	12		
Planting	6		
Weeding, 10 years ...	10		
Rent 10 years @ 2 Rs. an acre	20		
Rs...	64		
Interest of 9 years at 10 per cent. on 64 Rs. say...	54		
Felling 500 trees ...	30		
Carting 125 tons, at 2 Rs...	250		
Selling charges ...	60		
1st 10 years' charges ...	458		
Balance, Profit 10 years ...	542		
Rs...	1,000	Rs...	1,000
Rent, 30 years, at 2 Rs. ...	60	200 trees = 400 tons, at 8 Rs. a ton	3,200
Watching, &c., at 84 Rs. a year, for 20 years ...	1,640	200 trees, at 10,000 cubic feet, at 8 As. a foot ...	5,000
Felling 400 trees, at 8 As. ea.	200	100 trees, 40 years old, at 100 cubic feet, at 12 As. a cubic foot.	7,500
Do. 100 do. at 1 Rupee.	100	Tops of 100 trees, at 1 ton each, 8 Rs.	800
Carting 1,200 tons, at 2 Rs.	2,400		
Do. 100 do. at 2 Rs.	200		
Selling charges, &c, &c. ...	1,500		
Total charges ...	6,100		
Balance, Profit ...	10,942		
Rs...	17,042	Rs...	17,042

CHAPTER XII.

FUEL PLANTATIONS.

Prize Essay.*

Most suitable site for Plantations.—In considering the subject of sites for fuel plantations, we have to take into consideration the following points. First, proximity to large towns. Second, the distance from the coast or port, the nature of the land available, its proximity to good roads or water carriage. Assuming that the consumption is large, the most suitable site for a plantation, supposing such land is obtainable within five miles of a town, is low ground with a sandy soil, the water bearing strata being within six feet of the surface for the greater part of the year. In ground of this nature, numerous water holes can be sunk for watering the plants the first year, and in the second year, the roots will penetrate to the water bearing strata. In ground of this nature there is but one tree to plant, and that is† *casuarina muricata*. Its growth is exceedingly fast, and as fuel, its calorific powers are unsurpassed by any ordinary wood. It may be here remarked, that an especial condition for a fuel plantation is, that the tree should be fast-growing and one possessing high calorific powers, otherwise the plantation cannot pay. Having selected the site, let us plant it: first dig a water hole, make nurseries. It will save watering, if the seeds are mixed in a basket with damp sand for ten days, and then sown in lines in the nursery beds, the lines six inches apart, the seed being a light one requires but a slight covering of fine sand. The lines should be one inch deep, but the seed should only be

---

* By Major-General Morgan, Ootacamund.

† Some twenty years ago it was hotly debated in Madras, if *Inga dulcis* (Corkapilly) was not far superior to Casuarina for a firewood plantation. The first has no supporters now.

covered one quarter of an inch deep; fresh seed germinates more quickly than old; ripe seed produces better plants than green. Be very careful to select your seed from the strongest growing trees; should your lazy gardener go to a stunted tree loaded with seed and you use it, be sure your plantation must fail, as surely as if you had bred from a diseased and stunted animal; in nature, like produces like. Having sown your beds, cover them with pandals made of light brushwood to break the heat of the sun, water every evening and lightly, do not deluge your beds but keep the surface moist, in a few days the plant should appear above ground, when six inches high, shift them to another bed, having first carefully cut back the tap-root to four inches, to enable the plant to throw out bushy roots and thus take up more soil. A single root like a carrot takes up no soil, has no lateral roots for feeders, and once damaged recovers with difficulty; further when you plant out, there is no tap-root to turn up. Place your plants six inches apart in the beds, when they are one foot to eighteen inches in height, put them out into the pits. Select showery, cloudy weather, heavy rains are not good for planting out. The best time in most places is probably July. The plant then has six months before it to make roots before the dry weather sets in. The pits should be at least eighteen inches cube. In lifting plants from the beds, use a transplanter, they are far cheaper and quite as good as baskets. A cooly will carry a dozen at a time, and the plant is deposited in its pit without any disturbance of its roots, consequently there are no failures. On the careful lifting will depend the amount of watering they will require in the dry weather, for should they be safely deposited without any disturbance of their roots, they will go on growing and elongating their roots in search of water, and soon reach the desired object; whereas, if the roots are damaged, the plant has to renew them, and before this can be done, the hot weather arrives, and to keep it alive, heavy waterings are necessary. The plant should be put out 6 feet × 6 feet, this distance will allow of thinning out in the ninth year if the trees have grown well. In the first year the plants may require a slight shade of anything obtainable, such as grass, pieces of palmyra or cocoanut leaves, &c., shading will save watering. After the first year the young trees should take care of themselves. In the ninth year it will be necessary to thin the trees unless coppicing should be resorted to. I confess the thinning process seems to me to be the most paying process in the end, for the casuarina is not only a good firewood but a fair building timber, and by thinning out at the end of forty or fifty years, some good building timber would be available. Wight states "that the timber is without exception the strongest for bearing cross strains." In coppicing, it must be observed that all the trees are cut over at once, and all the stools have an equal start, but in thinning out, the shoots that come from the stools are poor, for the standing trees get the start of them and absorb an undue amount of food to the detriment of the coppiced stools. It may be mentioned that the ground being pure sand, there are no weeds. In the ninth year, the trees will have attained an average height of 60 feet with a diameter at the base of 8 inches tapering off to 4 inches at the top. In the Forest Report for 1872 and 1873, page 68: "The largest trees seven years old averaged 60 feet high and 30 inches in circumference at the ground, there are twenty thousand of them." At this age we proceed to coppice. Allowing for weakly trees and failures at 10 per cent. the returns may be taken as follows:—Five hundred trees full grown averaging 6 inches × 6 inches, for 50 feet = 12½ cubic feet a tree; then 500 trees × 12½ cubic feet = 6,250 cubic feet × 60 lbs. (weight of a cubic foot) = 375,000 lbs. and if we say half this weight for the other 500 trees, then we have for the acre 562,500 lbs., plus the tops which sell well as small wood, ten feet of tops equal 60 lbs. × 1,000 trees = 60,000 lbs. or in all 622,500 lbs. = 277 tons at 8 rupees a ton all round

= 2,216 rupees, for the acre. Then the account stands thus:—

Dr.

	RS.	A.	P.
To 1,250 plants at 5 per 1,000	6	4	0
Lining and 1,200 pits ...	7	0	0
Planting	6	0	0
Shading	2	8	0
Watering first year ...	16	0	0
Fencing	4	0	0
Rent	9	0	0
	50	12	0
9 years' interest at 10 per cent.	45	10	9
Cutting and lopping 100 trees	250	0	0
Carting 277 tons at 1-8-0	415	8	0
Expenses selling ...	76	0	0
Total...	837	14	9

Cr.

	RS.	A.	P.
Sale of 277 tons at 8 rupees	2,216	0	0
Deduct charges ...	837	14	9
Profit	1,378	1	3

Then from the total returns in the ninth year we have a profit of Rs. 1,378. I have not the slightest doubt that some of the casuarina plantations extending from Madras to near Pulicat realise the above profit, but not all; for it is a curious fact that the further from the surface the water is found, the more backward are the trees. And, probably, for trees growing inland, where the water-bearing stratum is, perhaps, ten feet from the surface, not more than half the above profit would be realised; but, after making every deduction for indifferent sites, and there is no place where the casuarina will not grow, except in stiff clay, it is, beyond comparison, the best tree to grow for a firewood plantation. If we assume that the trees are coppiced over once in ten years and that they give a return equal to the first cutting, then at the end of forty years the account will stand thus:—

Dr.

	RS.
Watching and pruning 10 years at Rs. 7 a month ...	840
Rent of land	10
Cutting and lopping 1,000 trees	250
Carting 277 tons at Rs. 1-8-0	416
Selling expenses	60
Total...	1,576
3rd ten years...	1,576
4th do. ...	1,576
Grand Total...	4,728

Cr.

	RS.
By balance profit	1,378
Sale of 277 tons at Rs. 8	2,216
Do. do. 30 years...	2,216
Do. do. 40 do. ...	2,216
Total...	8,026
Deduct charges...	4,728
Balance profit...	3,298

We will now treat the casuarina partly as a fuel, partly as a timber plantation. At the ninth year we shall cut out 500 trees equal to 375,000 lbs., plus tops = 30,000 lbs., total 405,000 lbs. = 180 tons at Rs. 8 = Rs. 1,440. From this we must deduct cost of planting.

Dr.	RS.	*Cr.*	RS.
Cost of planting as above ...	96	Sale of 180 tons at Rs. 8 ...	1,440
Cutting and lopping 500 trees...	125	Deduct charges	539
Carting 180 tons at Rs. 1-8-0 ...	270		
Selling charges	48	Balance profit...	901
Total...	539		

Here we have a profit to the tenth year of Rs. 901, and by gradual thinnings up to the thirtieth year, we can realise a revenue,—for to enable the last hundred trees on the acre to acquire their full growth, it will be necessary to take out 400 trees. If between the tenth and thirtieth year we take out an average of 20 trees a year, and assume that the first 20 trees contain an average of 25 cubic feet, and the last 20 trees an average of 50 cubic feet; then the mean of the 400 trees will be 37 cubic feet × 20 trees = 740 cubic feet, which if sold for building timber at only 6 annas a cubic foot, would bring every year for 20 years Rs. 278. Add value of tops for firewood at 300 lbs. a tree × 20 trees = 6,000 lbs. sold for firewood at Rs. 8 a ton = Rs. 21$\frac{3}{7}$ Then the account will stand as follows:—

Balance Sheet of 30 years of a Timber and Fuel Casuarina Plantation—

Dr.	RS.	*Cr.*	RS.
Watcher and feller at Rs. 7 a month for 20 years ...	1,680	Balance profit brought on ...	901
Carting 453 tons at Rs. 1-8-0	679	400 trees at 37 cubic feet each at 6 annas a cubic foot	5,550
Carting last 100 trees with tops = 180 tons at 1-8-0	270	Tops of 400 trees = 53½ tons at Rs. 8	428
Watcher and feller, 10 years, say Rs. 100	100	100 trees 40 years old = 60 cubic feet a tree, at As. 10 a cubic foot	3,750
Rent of land 30 years ...	30	Tops of 100 trees at 600 lbs. each, 8 Rs. a ton for 27 tons	216
Selling, &c., say 30 years ...	1,077	Total ...	10,845
Total ...	3,836	Deduct charges ...	3,836
		Balance profit ...	7,009

Here is a profit per acre shown of Rs. 7,009, and the returns are rather under-estimated, but it must be borne in mind that these are the returns for a good plantation. The data given above are founded on a practical basis, and no mere theory: the cost of planting, the growth of the trees, and the selling prices realized are all under-estimated, and the prices given can be realised in all large towns. With the exception of fuel plantations on the hills, it is simply waste of time and money to grow any tree but the casuarina for fuel plantations where the suitable sites are available. In forming the fuel plantation, I have omitted the description of the fence. Assuming the site to be sandy, a ditch three feet wide at top and six inches at bottom will be wide enough. The sand taken out should be placed on the inside of the ditch, on the top eighteen inches in width. Aloes, the croton oil plant or prickly euphorbia may be planted on the top. The ditch can be cheaply constructed for about 9 pies a running yard three feet deep. Any animal getting in will find a difficulty in getting out, as the shape of the bottom of the ditch will hedge him in. Prickly-pear should never be used, indeed spreading it in any way should be made penal, as they have made thistle-growing in Australia. It may be argued that the planting of casuarina is well understood and some other mode of forming fuel plantations should be pointed out. My reply is: The tree grows nearly everywhere and it is the best sort to grow. It is found from Madras on the East Coast to Calicut on the West; in dry plains, like the town of Bowani, and in moist places similar to Manantoddy, 2,500 feet above the sea. There are Eucalyptus plantations at our hill-stations, and I shall proceed to show how they are raised. The tree has not hitherto been found to grow well below 4,500 feet in any part of Southern India. No doubt there are some species of Eucalyptus growing in Queensland that might be found to succeed in Mysore and at elevations from 2,500 to 4,500 feet. The various kinds of Jarrah from West Australia grow best at 5,000 feet elevation;* the Tasmanian blue gum, *E. Globulus*, from 5,000 to 8,000 feet. To form a Eucalyptus plantation, first secure sholah-land, if possible, for the returns from sholah-land in the first ten years will be double those from grass-land. If sholah-land is not available, then secure grass-land facing the north with a good yellow sub-soil to retain the moisture. Make your nursery beds near water,—procure your seeds from the strongest trees. Sow in March in beds, the lines to be six inches apart, one inch deep; cover the seed half an inch deep, no more; water lightly; when the plants are six inches high, take up, cut back tap-roots to four inches, replant in beds six inches apart; when 12 to 18 inches high, take up with transplanter, and put out in pits, these should be 18 inches cubic. The young trees may be put out between June and September, selecting cloudy weather, if showery the better. Very heavy rain, or high wind, is bad for planting out. In placing the plant in the pit, press the earth well down, or the air will get to the roots and dry them up. If the trees are put out 6 feet × 6 feet, they must be thinned out in the ninth year. And as I have already shown that coppicing even for a fuel plantation does not pay, I shall show a balance sheet on the fuel and building timber basis. If we take the acre as holding 1,000 trees 50 feet high, and 12½ cubic feet each, then we cut out 500 trees in the ninth year at 12½ cubic feet each and 50 lbs. the cubic foot = 139½ tons, or to be within the mark, say 125 tons at Rs. 8 a ton = Rs. 1,000. The balance sheet shows expenses up to tenth year as Rs. 458; returns Rs. 1,000; profit Rs. 542. To show that the average weight of 625 lbs. a tree is not excessive, an eight-year old average tree out of a plantation was felled and weighed, it was found to exceed 1,600 lbs. A single *E. Globulus* tree about 40 years of age is known to contain 400 cubic feet of timber, which at 50 cubic feet the ton = 8 tons. This tree stands alone. In another place 25 trees of *E. Globulus* measure 9 feet in circumference at 6 feet from the

* The *Jarrah E. Marginata* might be found to grow well in Wynaad and similar climates.

ground and 3 feet at 100 feet in height, the total height being 140 feet. These 25 trees average 120 cubic feet each of good timber, and the trees are under 25 years of age. They occupy a space of one-sixth of an acre. Then 25 × 120 cubic feet = 3,000 cubic feet besides tops and branches. It is not possible for an acre to carry six times this quantity, because the roots of these trees occupy an acre of space. It must be added that, though these trees actually stand on 800 square yards or one-fourth of an acre, their roots may really occupy an acre, or even more. These examples will show to what growth *E. Globulus* may arrive at within 40 years. *E. Amygdalina*, the giant of the Australian forests, far exceeds this; 450 feet having been found to be the height of more than one tree. If we assume that between ten and thirty years, 400 trees are taken out and 100 left standing till 40 years old, and we take the mean of 400 trees at 50 cubic feet, (leaving 100 trees standing till 40 years old) being the mean of trees 10 to 30 years old, then we have for 400 trees of 50 cubic feet each, a total of 800 tons. Half of this amount at Rs. 8 a ton gives Rs. 3,200, the other half 400 tons at 8 annas a cubic foot for building purposes gives 400 tons × 25 cubic feet = 10,000 cubic feet at 8 annas = Rs. 5,000. If we take the last 100 trees at 40 years old as measuring 100 cubic feet each, we have 100 × 100 = 10,000 cubic feet at 12 annas = Rs. 7,500; tops and branches 1 ton each at Rs. 8 = Rs. 800 or in all Rs. 8,300. There is a great consumption of this wood for rafters, planks, reapers, and for building purposes. Ordinary woods sell for building teak, Rs. 2; vengay, Rs. 1-8-0; ven teak, Rs. 1-4-0 the cubic foot. Eucalyptus wood may be thoroughly seasoned in tanks in which unslaked lime has been placed in the proportion of one cubic foot of lime to six hundred of water; three months' soaking is enough for small scantlings, large beams require six months for the lime to permeate all the tubes and to be deposited,—for the theory is, that the sap is driven out and the lime water takes its place. Of course, all timber should be felled at the wane of the moon, and in December, January and February. *Acacia molissima* makes a good firewood, but does not grow so rapidly as the Eucalyptus; it has much tar in it and burns green but is not suited for building timber and it has an objectionable habit of throwing up suckers from its roots. The Eucalyptus could be treated as coppice but would not pay so well. I annex a balance sheet to show the profit of an acre of Eucalyptus at the end of 40 years. In grass-land the profit would be one-half. It is understood that much depends on judicious thinning, not to take out strong trees to allow weak ones to come on, as is sometimes done, for it must be clearly understood that a strong tree is always a strong tree, but it does not follow that a weak tree will grow into a strong tree by having room given to it to expand. There may be other causes than want of root space which retard its growth, such as inherent constitutional weakness, poor soil, incipient disease, &c.

Balance Sheet of an Acre of Eucalyptus from 1st to 40th year—

Dr.	RS.	*Cr.*	RS.
Clearing ground	10	Sale of 500 trees, 125 tons at	
Plants 1,200	6	Rs. 8 a ton	1,000
Pits 1,200	12	Deduct charges	461
Planting	6		
Weeding	10	Balance profit ...	539
Rent 10 years	20	200 trees = 400 tons at Rs. 8 ...	3,200
		200 trees at 50 cubic feet =	
Interest 9 years	64	10,000 cubic feet at 8 annas	
Felling 500 trees ...	57	a foot	5,000
	30	100 trees at 100 cubic feet at	
Carting 125 tons at Rs. 2 ...	250	annas 12*	7,500
Selling charges	60	Tops of 100 trees 1 ton each at	
		Rs. 8	800
Total...	461		
		Total ...	17,039
Rent 30 years at Rs. 2 ...	60	Deduct charges ...	6,140
Watching at Rs. 84 a year for 20 years	1,680	Balance profit ...	10,899
Felling 400 trees at annas 8...	200		
Felling 100 trees at R. 1 ...	100		
Carting 1,200 tons at Rs. 2 ...	2,400		
Carting 100 tons at Rs. 2 ...	200		
Selling charges, &c.	1,500		
Total ...	6,140		

* 100 cubic feet are under the mark, but I have thought it better to keep the average at this.

I now proceed to annex a balance sheet of a Teak fuel and timber plantation. The wood has high calorific properties from the quantity of oil it contains, and it makes excellent charcoal. Teak timber near the coast always brings a good price. We will assume that a good site is chosen on the banks of a river navigable to the sea on the western coast. A few miles more or less of water-carriage do not affect the profits of firewood, nor, indeed, does railway carriage; for at 8 pies a ton a mile, fuel may be carried 30 miles without disturbing the profits, as fuel can always afford to pay Rs. 1-8-0 a ton for carriage. Teak can be treated as coppice but, as shown above, the returns do not equal the fuel and timber system.

Balance Sheet of a Teak Fuel and Timber Plantation 40 years—

Dr.	RS.	A.	P.	*Cr.*	RS.	A.	P.
Clearing grounds per acre	10	0	0	Sale of 500 poles at 8 annas each ...	250	0	0
Pitting 1,200 pits ...	12	0	0	Deduct charges...	238	0	0
Plants 1,200	6	0	0				
Weeding 10 years ...	25	0	0	Balance profit ...	12	0	0
Ten years' rent at Rs. 2 per acre	20	0	0	400 trees 10 to 30 years old averaging 20 cubic feet at 1 R.	8,000	0	0
Total ...	73	0	0				
Nine years' interest at 10 per cent. ...	65	0	0	100 trees at 40 cubic feet at 1-4-0 per cubic foot... ...	5,000	0	0
Total ...	138	0	0	Tops for firewood and charcoal, 500 trees at 1 ton each at 8 Rs.	4,000	0	0
Felling 500 trees ...	30	0	0				
Floating to Depôt 33 tons, say	50	0	0				
Selling	20	0	0	Total...	17,012	0	0
Total...	238	0	0	Deduct charges ...	5,530	0	0
To care of trees for 20 years at Rs. 84 a year, felling included	1,680	0	0	Balance...	11,482	0	0
Floating or carting 8,000 cwt. at 2 annas	1,000	0	0				
Felling and squaring 100 trees at 1 R. ...	100	0	0				
Carting 4,000 cubic feet at 2 annas ...	500	0	0				
Carriage 500 tons firewood at Rs. 1-8-0 per ton	750	0	0				
Selling charges, &c...	1,500	0	0				
Total ...	5,530	0	0				

It will be seen from the above balance sheet that there are few more profitable investments than a Teak plantation* near the coast and a large town ; but then very few suitable sites are to be found, and where casuarina would flourish, Teak would languish even on the western coast.

Fuel plantation of a reserved jungle.—We have now to consider a fuel plantation of a reserved jungle, such as Streehurrycotta, which at one time, before the formation of casuarina plantations, supplied all Madras with fuel, or we may take some of the fuel reserves along the line of Railway. Having selected the site, which should be close to a Railway or possess water-carriage like the Buckingham Canal, make a ditch with a fence at the top for the casuarina plantation ; but instead of aloes it will be necessary to plant the Mysore thorn, *cœsalpinia digyna,* (*acacia scandens?*) which will present an impenetrable barrier to marauding cattle. The block should be nearly a square, as that shape saves fencing. The area should not be less than one square mile, because to produce any local effect on the atmosphere, and to be of any use at all as a fuel plantation, at least 600 acres are required. We will suppose the area to be partly covered with various trees, such as acacias, *eugenias,* &c., most of the young trees considerably damaged by cattle and the herdsman's bill-hook, and more grass growing than is good for their health. It is of no use commencing operations until the ditch and fence are completed, for, in the dry season, nothing will keep out herdsmen or their cattle but the thorniest of fences, and there is no thorn like the Mysore thorn. Aloes can be cut through in a moment and only serve as a defence where there is nothing tempting inside. The fence completed, it is necessary to take stock of the standing trees. It is found that about half the area is covered, and that the other half requires artificial aid to render the area productive. This being a semi-natural plantation, we shall treat it in the simplest manner, spending but

* On the western coast in planting out Teak, the trees are taken straight from the beds when six inches high, and put into pits after their tap-roots have been cut back to four inches.

little money on it, and assisting nature as much as possible. Many of these natural scrub jungles appear to be thickly wooded; but directly they are cut into, it is surprising to find how little wood they really contain. Where an artificial plantation of thirty years of age will contain 4 or 500 tons of wood per acre, the natural jungle crowded with umbrella-shaped trees will scarcely produce 100 tons. What we require is a tall tree carrying plenty of wood, and occupying but a small space, or, that the acre shall carry two to three hundred tons instead of one hundred. It will be necessary to dig a well in some favorable spot, as it is intended when the soil is very favorable, and facilities for watering are available, that nursery plants should be put in; as these spots will be rare, we must adopt another style of planting for the greater part of the fuel plantation. On the square mile we shall keep a head gardener and two men. It will be their duty to trim and lop trees, and cut out where the trees are too thick, (as it is as bad to have the trees too crowded as to have too few). They will put out plants, keep the hedge in order, make charcoal, dig holes, and put out seeds in the proper season. It may appear a very simple matter to drop a seed into a hole and leave it to grow; but, unless due precautions are taken, not five per cent. of the seeds will grow, and we require at least 90 per cent. of the seeds to succeed. There is one advantage in planting by seeds,—that we can always put out three or four thousand seeds to the acre and then cut out the surplus plants; but where plants are put out singly in pits and require to be watered the first year, to plant close becomes a very expensive process, nor is there anything gained by it. The best mode of planting seeds *in situ* is as follows:—On the first heavy rain, when the ground is soft, let the men go round with the crowbars and make holes six inches deep and as wide as possible by working the crowbar backwards and forwards; the holes to be three feet apart. Prepare your seed by keeping it in damp-sand, exposed to a hot sun until it germinates. In the meantime if another shower has fallen, the holes will be partially filled in by earth having been washed in. Then one man proceeds with a basket of damp-sand in which are the germinated seeds, and drops a seed in each hole, taking care that the seeds are not more than one inch from the surface. Should the holes be still open, two men should scrape a little damp-earth into the hole, the last man covers the seed. By planting in damp weather with germinated seed, two objects are gained; first, the certainty that the seed grows, second, that at least two months are saved. Thus if the seed is put in with the first heavy rain of the year, it grows rapidly and has all the north-east monsoon before it, whereas if not germinated before planting, it may be two months or more before it comes up, and the monsoon be lost. Many acacia seeds refuse to germinate for months, and require to be soaked 24 hours in hot water; but very damp sand is, as a rule, the best for keeping the seeds in, especially if exposed to a hot sun. The seed should not be prepared until a short time before you are ready to plant, say ten to twenty days, for as soon as the seed germinates, which may be known in most seeds by a small white radicle appearing at one end of the seed, it should then be planted or the radicle may be broken. Having planted our seed, it must be left to nature to do the rest, we cannot afford any more artificial treatment. Very small seeds, such as casuarina, should be planted in beds and treated as in artificial plantations. Trees good for charcoal and fuel only, should be planted,—*Jannesabit, Acacia Arabica, A. oderatissima, Speciosa, Ferruginea, Cassia floribunda, Inga dulcis,* Eugenia sorts, Neem, Jack, Casuarina. These will be sufficient for the fuel reserve,—they all give good results and grow fast. If water is near the surface, it would be of advantage to sink a few chatty wells. Wudders will sink these, not more than three feet diameter, for a small sum, and they last a long time. When not otherwise engaged, the gardeners should be employed in thinning out, making room for promising plants to come on, and by no means allowing the trees to overcrowd each other, and to encourage them to assume a vertical habit of growth by trimming occasionally. With care most trees can be drawn up. Something must now be said of the making of charcoal which is always worth 30 rupees a ton, for that which is really good. This price gives nearly 6 rupees a ton for the wood without carriage, the extra labour for making charcoal being met by the saving in cost of carriage; for instance, 4 tons of wood = 32 rupees, minus carriage of 3 tons = 4-8-0, this goes to pay for making the charcoal which, made in the native fashion, is fearfully destructive of jungle.* I shall show the proper way to make it, by which mode 4 tons of wood produce 1 ton of charcoal, and it may be here observed that the calorific powers of various kinds of charcoal differ quite as much as wood. It may be laid down as a rule, that the heaviest woods produce the best charcoal, sal weighing 90 lbs. a cubic foot makes the best. Charcoal requiring to be made in different places, it is better to have a portable kiln rather than bring the wood to a permanent structure. The kiln is made of sheet iron; it is 9 feet high, 10 feet in diameter at bottom and 5 feet at the top; at the bottom 1 foot from the ground are a number of circular holes 6 inches in diameter, closed with sliding doors; there is a circular hole in the top closed in the same manner. When the fire is well alight below, the holes are closed one by one, and when the fire has got to the top, that hole is closed. All chinks are carefully plastered over, the kiln remains closed four or five days until all signs of fire have departed. It is then opened out; first the top is taken off, then the sides are unbolted, and the whole of the contents on being laid bare are found to be a mass of charcoal of the best kind. A stack of wood is built in another suitable place, the kiln set up and bolted together. In this way with half-a-dozen kilns going, a large amount of charcoal may be turned out, with but small loss. The cost of the iron kilns is heavy, about 150 rupees: they will last many years. In the balance sheet prepared,

* Colonel Beddome, in a report to Government, February 1876, No. 302, writes of "7 or 8 loads of wood to make a ton of charcoal." Probably he meant 7 or 8 tons of wood.

no mention is made of charcoal, but the wood can always be made into charcoal, and the cost of making it is met by the saving of the carriage of the wood. Really good charcoal will always bring 30 rupees a ton,—that made in iron kilns is always superior to that made in holes in the ground and deluged with water; the one looks bright and glossy black, the other dull and a grey black. In Salem and in Kurnool, where native iron is largely made, the saving to the jungles, by making charcoal in a scientific manner, would be very great. The native fashion certainly causes a waste of from 75 to 100 per cent.

Balance Sheet of a Fuel Plantation for 20 years.

Dr.	RS.	*Cr.*	RS.
One head gardener and 2 men at 10 Rs. + 6 Rs. = for 1 year 264 × 20 years.	5,280	10th year 640 tons at Rs. 8	5,120
8,000 yards trench at 1 anna per running yard	500	10 to 20 years, average of fuel per acre, 15 tons on 640 acres at 8 Rs. ...	76,800
12 Chatty wells at 20 rupees	240	Total...	81,920
Gardener's hut Rs. 50, tools Rs. 30	80	Deduct charges...	41,760
6 Charcoal iron kilns at 150 .	900	Profit on 20 years...	40,160
Carriage 640 tons at 1-8-0 ...	960		
Carriage 9,600 tons at 1-8-0 .	14,400		
Selling charges, supervision, &c.	10,000		
Rent for 20 years at 8 annas per acre	6,400		
Interest 10 per cent. for 5 years on Rs. 6,000... ...	3,000		
Total charges in 20 years. .	41,760		

The profit shown after deducting all charges is about 3 rupees an acre a year. This by superior supervision might easily be increased, or by inferior supervision be turned into a loss. I attach the greatest importance to skilled supervision. I shall now discuss the vexed question of tap-roots, as so much has been written on the subject and so great stress laid on the preservation of them, that I feel it is incumbent on me to show why, in most cases, they must be cut, and why nature has given to certain plants powerful tap-roots and to others none. I shall show the uses of the tap-root and why certain plants can do without them, but to others it is a necessity. The soil, the situation, the climate, the habit of the tree, all go to show, why in one place the tree requires a tap-root and in another place can dispense with it. When seeds are planted *in situ* and cannot be watered on account of the expense, it is evident they must depend entirely on their roots for nourishment, and to gain moisture one or more of their roots must be plunged deep into the earth beyond the action of the sun's rays. Let us take the tamarind tree for an example. Nature has furnished it with a powerful tap-root to enable it to exist in dry places. Very frequently, the tap-root will be nearly a yard long when the head of the plant is not six inches high. To expect to lift a plant with a root so long is simply hopeless, it must be damaged more or less. If, when the plant is lifted, the tap-root is shortened by a clean cut, and the plant put back into a bed and watered, it rapidly makes lateral roots and is then fit for lifting with the transplanter. When put out in the pit, it must be watered if the situation is dry and the rains cannot be depended on for any length of time. It is otherwise in moist places, where the rains can be depended on for weeks. In such places cuttings of trees thrust in the ground root freely. No one thinks of watering tea, coffee, cinchona, teak, or eucalyptus plants, because they are put out under favorable circumstances; but where the conditions are unfavourable, we must water or trust entirely to nature by planting the seeds *in situ* and leaving the tap-root to do its work. Many seeds, if planted in sandy soil or fibrous peaty soil, do not throw out a single tap-root at all but a number of lateral roots, provided the ground is kept moist. I have known tea plants in one bed full of peat throw out any amount of lateral roots, and in an adjoining bed where the clay was near the surface, send down one single tap-root like a carrot. The roots in the first bed found a soil suitable for supplying food to many roots, in the second case the plant had to send down a single long tap-root to get food as there was none near at hand. It is a well established fact that the tap-root after three or four years ceases to grow, having performed the functions intended for it by nature, and being no longer required, a number of lateral roots take its place, and if they do not find moisture near the surface, plunge deep down for it. No one ever saw a tree blown over in a forest with a tap-root to it, or the sign of one. I have examined hundreds of trees. Sometimes in natural moist forests it is almost impossible to walk for the roots that cover the surface in a perfect net work. I have seen miles of banyan trees blown down and not even a lateral root penetrating the earth, showing how much this tree in a dry climate derives its moisture from the air. Many years ago, in a storm that swept down miles of avenue trees between Trichinopoly and Coimbatore, the uprooted trees presented a vast hollow centre where the tap-root usually appears. Observe a banyan tree growing out of a palmyra tree or out of the cleft in a wall of a ruined pagoda. Where is its tap-root? No where! The roots are seen like those of an orchid clinging to the wall or tree. There are many trees that exist not so much by the moisture the roots pump up from the earth, as by the moisture the leaves absorb from the atmosphere. Those not capable of absorbing moisture from the atmosphere, part with none through their leaves, such as the casuarina and eucalyptus, both calculated by the shape and texture of their leaves to withstand dry winds. Observe the Teak tree, its vast leaves will only enable it to flourish in moist places, as the amount of evaporation exercised on such an extent of leaf area would soon exhaust it in a dry climate. Nature always provides a remedy, and if one tree has no deep roots, it is enabled to absorb moisture from the atmosphere; if it cannot absorb moisture then it loses none. Again, by capillary attraction moisture in the earth is always rising to the surface, and thus many roots obtain a supply. If it were possible to take up a plant with a long tap-root without injury, then it would be advisable to do so, but as it is a simple impossibility to take up a plant of any size without damage, we are forced to cut the tap-root. Even in planting small Teak, tea or coffee plants, if the tap-root is over six inches, it is almost certain to be turned up, and then it cannot possibly grow. When the tap-root has been turned up, it may at once be known and the tree picked out of a thousand. So little is the question of the treatment of tap-roots understood that a crude experiment made by a Sub-Conservator in Bengal was actually sent down to the Madras Forest Department as a kind of guide. The deduction arrived at by the Sub-Conservator was, that "cutting tap-roots when the plant was strong (query, large?) was advisable, but if the plant was weak (small?) they should not be cut"; if he had added that the weakly plants should be thrown away, he would have been right. There is no more fatal error than putting out weak plants; at the best they make but indifferent trees. It is astonishing to see the number of weakly seedlings that come up in a bed, though some care may have been taken in securing good seed, especially where seeds are small, such as cinchona or casuarina seeds.

Concluding Remarks.

In recommending the use of the transplanter, I have carefully considered its advantages over moss, baskets, peat pots, flower pots and bamboos, indeed, have tried them all; but for simplicity, economy and certainty, nothing can equal the transplanter. In using it, if the soil is light and dry, a copious watering should be given to the beds, and the earth round the plants pressed down, so that the earth may not fall away from the roots. A native, in planting out, if left alone, exemplifies the way of how not to do it. First, he tears the plants out of the beds by main force; making them into a bundle, he grasps them by the roots, any that he cannot hold, are carefully laid down in the sun; in planting he uses a dibble, grasps a plant out of the bundle drawing the roots forcibly through his left hand, places the root in the small hole made by the dibble, carefully turning up the tap-root as he does so, then stamps down the earth on the top leaving the sides open—thus the plant is put out, and, I need hardly say, killed. With a transplanter, all this is impossible. In calculating the quantity of fuel to be obtained from a fuel reserve, planted up, I have estimated the yield from the tenth to twentieth year at 15 tons the acre, though I find that Colonel Beddome, in a Report to Government, only estimated the yield of ordinary scrub jungle at half a ton an acre yearly. Here there is a great discrepancy, but it must be observed in the Report under consideration the jungle in question had not been planted up or conserved in any way, *viz.*, fenced, and cattle and fires kept out, whereas my fuel plantation has been carefully conserved and planted up for fifteen years. If we consider what half a ton means, the estimate appears surprisingly low. Ordinary trees make a cubic foot of wood a year, but allowing for a dry climate and poor soil half a cubic foot a year is a fair average, or say 25lbs. and allow only 300 trees the acre, this gives us an annual increment of a little more than three tons an acre a year. I think this is nearer the mark, and if we plant up and really conserve the jungle, a yield of 15 tons a year per acre after the trees are ten years old, is not too high. It is understood that the process of cutting out, and renewal by seed-planting, goes on in a uniform manner.

Calorific powers of wood.

As there is much uncertainty regarding the calorific powers of various kinds of wood, I append a short table showing how woods vary in their value as fuel.

Beech wood split and dry ...	1·0
Red pine	0·61
Poplar	0·50
White pine	0·72
Oak wood (Summer)	1·18

It may safely be assumed that casuarina, Teak and many of our acacias have a greater calorific power than any in the list here shown, and the difference between beech and poplar proves how necessary it is that a fuel plantation should only consist of the best fuel trees. It is well known to Engineers, that with inferior fuel steam cannot be kept up, and on the Railway they have ample experience of various kinds of fuel, *Acacia sundra* bearing an excellent reputation and *Pongamia glabra* the reverse. It is the same with charcoal, no blacksmith will use any charcoal but that made from *E. Jamboolana* sál, Teak or hard and heavy Acacia wood. *Eucalyptus globulus* is also esteemed. I have given examples of the growth of this tree; some imagine that the faster the tree grows the worse the wood is. Even Loudon is not free from this idea. On page 647 " Encyclopædia of Agriculture," he writes, that " a certain slowness of growth is essentially necessary to the closeness of texture and durability". . . but Lindley (" Theory of Horticulture" page 415,) maintains that " fast grown timber is the strongest." It is a well-known fact amongst experienced arboriculturists that in places where the soil, climate and elevation is suitable, fast grown Teak is the best, but in low, swampy situations, fast grown Teak is apt to be spongy. For instance, Palghaut Teak cannot be compared with Anamallay or Wynaad. Nor can the Teak grown in low situations in Burmah be compared with that grown in the Attaram Forests. Timber really derives its goodness from the soil, not from its rate of growth. Given a good soil, good situation, and good climate, the tree must grow fast and produce good timber; let any of these be wanting, and the result is spongy or knotted and twisted timber of slow growth and small. It is rather a puzzle to know where the casuarina grown in pure sand obtains its hard timber. Silica and water it has in abundance, but the lime potash and other ingredients that go to build up a tree,—where do they come from? The answer is, they must be in the water. For instance, rain falls inland on high ground: then by percolation is carried down through various strata until it can sink no lower; then by underground passages it finds its way for miles, it may be ten or a thousand! finally, no longer repressed by rocks or beds of clay it rises by syphonic* action to the surface,

* We have an excellent example of this syphonic action in the celebrated rock of Ghoty which rises some 1,000 feet high out of the plain and

bringing with it all the various ingredients derived from the strata through which it has percolated. It may be argued that in this Essay I have paid more attention to timber than to fuel plantations, but I answer in the words of Lindley, "Fast grown timber is the strongest" whether it be for fuel or building purposes, and I would add that in all cases, where practicable, always select the best soils for a plantation rather than indifferent ones. I must here mention that on no account should the same kind of tree be planted to fill up vacancies in the fuel reserve; for instance, *acacia sundra* is common in scrub jungle growing rather far apart. To fill in the vacancies put in seeds of tamarind, E. jamboolana, neem, and jack; for one kind of tree invariably consumes all the food in its vicinity required for its special conditions. This is well exemplified in the Teak plantations at Nellumbore, where occasionally a natural Teak tree is observed to have been enclosed in the artificial Teak plantation; for a radius of thirty feet all the young Teak languishes and refuses to grow, but should a blackwood tree have been enclosed, the young Teak near it flourishes and does not exhibit any appearance of poverty.

The old Scotch adage declares that "Hawks do not pike out Hawks e'en," but assuredly old trees of the same species devour their young; for instance, the wild cinnamon has a large seed which rapidly germinates, thousands of young plants may be seen around the parent tree, growing well so long as the food in the seed supports the young plant, which may be for six months; by the end of a year there is hardly a young plant alive. The same results take place with the wild mango.

After the whole block has been felled over at the end of the tenth year, a dense crop of suckers will come up. This is due to the light being let in.

---

half way up are deep wells in the rock; also in the seashore from Madras to Pulicat fresh water is found in the sandy strip of land close to the sea near the surface, and inland but a short distance, where beds of clay prevail, brackish water is found.

If in any portion of the block there is a paucity of suckers, it is advisable to cut shallow trenches across the bare spots, parallel to one another, and at intervals of from four to six feet apart so as to sever the roots of the trees cut over. This will immediately produce an abundant supply. The suckers may be left alone now for two years, when, if the soil is fairly good, they will have made such growth that they may be thinned out to six feet apart, the most vigorous being left, and the weakly ones cut away.

At the end of the fourteenth year the sucker growth may be cut over; but the entire block, or a portion, should be completely cleared, in order that light may be let in, and a new crop of suckers spring up.

The roots of the trees cut over in the first crop having taken complete possession of the soil, the second crop ought to produce twice as much as the first, and in fact will do so.

The third crop of suckers will produce five-eighths more than the original planting and afterwards this will be about the average septennial produce. No other description of tree that I know of will continue to produce heavy crops of fuel for a great number of consecutive years as this one will, for it is almost impossible to eradicate it when once thoroughly established, and it should, therefore, never be grown on, soil which is to be devoted afterwards to other crops.

It is desirable in making a wattle plantation to plant a few * *E. Globulus* trees between, as they considerably add to the outturn of the first two crops, the Eucalyptus being felled over from the stool at the end of the fourteenth year when the stool-shoot will be of considerable size—on an average, fourteen inches in diameter and sixty feet high.

As I have known of no instances of *E. Globulus* being felled over more than twice from the stool, I cannot say how often it would bear this treatment. Any assertion on this head would be mere theory; but it can, I think, be safely

* Mr. Laserson's Fuel Plantation on the Segur road is an instance of this.

expected, that it would stand the shock of being cut down five or six times in as many septennial fellings without showing any considerable diminution of outturn.

In making mixed plantations of Eucalyptus and Acacias, it must, however, be borne in mind that the former must be planted far apart, twenty or thirty feet at least, as otherwise they would, by their superior rate of growth, injure or destroy the less vigorous, and more slowly growing Acacias.

To form a plantation of *Eucalyptus Globulus,* shola or fern land is the best. If possible, a north-easterly aspect should be chosen, especially in the case of grass-land where the south-west monsoon impoverishes the soils that have that aspect from the constant denudation and wash that take place, which carries all the humus down to the valleys. It is, therefore, the *bottoms* of the valleys where the *E. Globulus* will flourish best and attain its maximum height. The largest tree of this species on the Nílgiris is to be found in such a situation, and at Gayton Park, it is over fourteen feet in circumference at six feet from the ground.* The next largest is to be found at Woodcock Hall, and is thirteen feet eight inches at three feet from the ground. This latter grows on grass-land, the former in Shola.

I estimate the Gayton Park tree to contain 400 cubic feet, of timber equal to eight tons and worth Rs. 64. It is about forty years old. Of course it could not be expected that many trees would reach this size even in a timber plantation at forty years, for this particular one has the monopoly of the soil all round, standing as it does, by itself.

A blue-gum-tree, twenty-five years of age, growing amongst others even larger, produced 120 cubic feet, and I shall base my calculations on this outturn.

Having obtained a block of rich shola-land, a small piece should be selected for a nursery.

It is necessary to have water near, or be able to divert it to the spot. The ground, if steep, should be terraced or

* This tree is said to be thirty years old.

thrown into beds, if level, and each bed to be 3½ feet broad, and from 10 to 30 feet long.

The seed obtained from the best and most mature trees should be sown early in March, for, if put down in January or February, the young plants may be cut down by frost.

It should not be buried deeper than three-eighths of an inch, and should be in rows about 6 or 7 inches apart.

When the young plants are 9 inches high, they should be taken out, and the tap-root cut to a length of not more than 4½ inches, so that lateral rootlets may be thrown out all round. This is done with a two-fold object. In the first place, the Canarese or other cooly, if left to his own devices, is certain, in planting out, to trust the wretched plant into the pit anyhow. The consequence is, that the long tap-root gets doubled back, and the plant languishes and dies, or, if it does succeed in growing at all, only produces a mis-shapen, stunted, weakly tree. When, however, the tap-root has been cut, innumerable fibrous roots are thrown out in every direction, principally laterally, and these seize upon and extract the nourishment which they find in the surface humus thrown into the pit.

After the tap-root has been shortened, the plant should be put either into a small bamboo basket, or tied up with humus round the roots, and wrapped in a bit of old gunny bag or moss, and tied round with "*Nar*" (bark). It can then be replaced in the bed.

In the first burst of the monsoon these young plants, which, by that time, will have grown to a height of 12 to 18 inches, will have thrust their roots through the fibrous covering which envelopes them below. They are now ready for planting out.

Of course, by this time the provident planter has had his land cleared, burnt, lined, and pitted 6 feet × 6 feet, also fenced.* He only waits for the first burst of the monsoon, when the ground has been thoroughly saturated. Coolies

---

* A line of acacias 6 feet deep ought to surround every Eucalyptus plantation to keep the wind out.

are now employed all day long in planting out. Each pit is half filled by scraping in the rich, dark-brown humus lying round, *not* the yellow sub-soil that has been taken, perhaps, out of the bottom of the pit. The ball of moss-covered earth, protecting the roots, is gently placed on the soil thus cast in, and fresh humus thrown in and firmly pressed down all round. If the plants are small, a few large clods should be placed round, to partially break the force of the monsoon-gale.

About the tenth* year, it will be necessary to thin out the crop, if it is desired to form a mixed fuel and timber plantation; but not otherwise.

The best distance to plant Eucalyptus is undoubtedly 6 feet × 6 feet. This will give 1,200 trees to the acre, and at ten years of age they ought to average † three trees to the ton or produce a total of 400 tons at Rs. 8 per ton = Rs. 3,200.

The following balance sheet will show the profit on the transaction per acre:—

Statement C—10 years.

Expenditure.	RS.	Receipts, &c.	RS.
Felling, burning, &c.	12	By sale of 400 tons at Rs. 8 per ton	3,200
Pitting at 25 pits per day per man, earning 4 annas cooly, 1,200 pits	12	Expenditure	1,157
Plants	5	Profit	2,043
Transplanting	7		
Sickling weeds...	10		
Tax at Rs. 2 per acre... ...	20		
	66		
Interest at 10 per cent. for 10 years	66		
Felling and lopping 1,200 trees at 3 annas per tree ...	225		
Carting 400 tons at Rs. 2 per ton	800		
Total ...	1,157		

* Sometimes as early as the fifth.

† A ten-year old will produce a ton, if growing by itself, and in rich soil.

A plantation of this kind can be advantageously coppiced, for *E. Globulus* shoots freely from the stool, and in the second decennial felling, will produce a considerably heavier crop than during the first, as the tree has already an abundance of well-formed, far-reaching roots, all in active operation, in providing the growing stool-shoot with sap; whereas the original seedlings had to spend considerable time in taking possession of the ground with its roots. As I have already stated, how long this system of coppicing with the Eucalyptus will pay, is purely a matter of conjecture. I shall proceed now to give the result of working a mixed timber and fuel plantation of Eucalyptus.

Having established your plantation in the manner already set forth, it will be necessary in the tenth year to make the first thinning, and we can then cut out 50 per cent. of the more weakly trees, to make room for the rest. The trees thus cut over will shoot from the stool, but the shoots will be poor and weakly, owing to the shade of the ones left.

The trees felled can be cut up into billets at about 3 annas per tree and sold for firewood.

In the fifteenth year, a second thinning will be necessary, and 220 trees should then be felled and lopped at a cost of 6 annas each and sold for fuel.

In the twentieth year, a third and last thinning may be carried out, of another 220 of the least vigorous trees remaining, leaving 160 of the largest, at as even distances as possible apart, for timber.

This thinning can be sold for timber and should fetch 6 annas per cubic foot, but I will only take its value as fuel.

At the end of the twenty-fifth year, the balance may be felled for timber. The trees will then average 110 cubic feet each, and realise ten annas per cubic foot in the market.

The balance sheet for twenty-five years for an acre of

mixed timber and fuel plantation of *E. Globulus* will therefore be as follows :—

Expenditure.	RS.	A.	P.
Felling and lopping 600 trees at 3 annas each	112	8	0
Felling 220 trees at 6 annas each	82	8	0
Carting 220 trees of $1\frac{1}{2}$ tons each = 330 tons, at Rs. 2 per ton	660	0	0
Felling 220 trees at 12 annas each ...	165	0	0
Carting 220 trees of 2 tons each=440 tons, at Rs. 2 per ton ...	880	0	0
Felling 160 trees of 110 cubic feet each at 1-4 per tree ...	200	0	0
Carting 160 trees of above dimensions= $392\frac{6}{7}$ tons at Rs. 2 per ton	785	11	5
Expenditure up to 10 years as per Statement C	1,157	0	0
Add * rent up to 25 years	30	0	0
Simple interest for 15 years on all expenditure up to the tenth year at 10 per cent...	1,735	8	0
Total ...	5,808	3	5
Add supervision and sundries at 10 per cent.	580	13	$1\frac{7}{10}$
Grand Total of Expenditure	6,389	0	$6\frac{7}{10}$

Receipts.	RS.	A.	P.
Sale of 600 trees at Rs. 8 per ton=200 tons	1,600	0	0
Add simple interest at 10 per cent. for 15 years on value recovered from plantation in the tenth year, Rs. 1,600 ...	2,400	0	0
330 tons of fuel from second thinning at Rs. 8 per ton ...	2,640	0	0
440 tons of fuel from third felling at Rs. 8 per ton	3,520	0	0
17,600 cubic feet of timber from 160 trees, 110 cubic feet each, of last felling at 10 annas per cubic foot	11,000	0	0
Total	21,160	0	0
Deduct Charges ...	6,389	0	$6\frac{7}{10}$
Profit Rs. ...	14,770	15	$5\frac{3}{10}$

I have drawn out the above statement on the supposition that the owner leaves his plantation to a certain extent to nature, having charged nothing against the pay of a watchman, or made any provision for charges connected with the sale of the timber, &c. A watchman is only necessary to prevent grass fires damaging the trees, or any one hacking,

* 10 years' rent has been calculated in the previous statement.

or stealing them. If, however, provision is made for a watchman, a sum of Rs. 170, at Rs. 12 per acre annually, would have to be charged to this head, and selling charges would come to about a thousand rupees, and these two items would lower the profit to Rs. 13,600-0-5$\frac{3}{10}$ per acre for the twenty-five years.

Mixed Fuel Reserves.—Supposing a man were to become possessed of 500 acres of natural jungle, what would be the most profitable method of working it, if it were near a large town?

In the first place, such a block would most probably consist of a mixture of trees, many species of which would be of little or no value as fuel.

I will here give a list of a few such trees, as it may be of service in teaching the fuel planter what *not* to plant:—

	Tamil.	
Pongamia glabra ...	Poonga Maram.	புங்கமரம்.
Bombax Malabarica.	Mool Ellavay Maram.	முள்இலவமரம்.
Erythrina Indica ...	Moorkoo Maram ...	முருக்கமரம்.
Semecarpus Anacardium.	Seyrankottay Maram.	சேராங்கொட்டைமரம்.
Ficus of all species.	Athie Marangul ...	அத்திமரங்கள்.
Terminalia Bellerica.	Thani Maram ...	தானிமரம்.
Mallotus Peltata ...	Uppu Kutthi Maram.	உப்புகுத்திமரம்.
&c. &c. &c.		

The first thing to be done would be to cut down and get rid of such trees, thorny bushes, and brushwood as uselessly encumber the ground to the detriment of more valuable fuel-producers, and dispose of them for what they will fetch. The poorer classes of natives will be glad enough to purchase for a trifle such stuff, and will remove it themselves. It will be necessary to exercise proper supervision when this is being done, or damage may be committed.

Where the soil is but scantily covered with trees, it will be advisable to fell out and sell such, in order that there may be no interference by mature trees with young ones planted out.

It is here necessary to caution the amateur fuel-planter against attempting to stock his jungle by planting out seedlings under grown-up trees. This will assuredly fail, as I have already explained.

The block should be thoroughly fenced round, and the cheapest and best permanent fence I know of, is one to be formed in the following manner:—

A deep ditch, with the bottom wedge-shaped, 4 feet deep and 4 feet wide, is to be excavated, the earth being thrown up on the inner side. A fence of the same description as that provided for a casuarina plantation, previously described by me, should now be erected on the summit of the thrown-up earth; and when the croton has struck, germinated seeds of palmyra (*Borassus flabelliformis*) should be sown at intervals of 4 feet on the inner side of the hedge. These, when grown up, make a splendid fence, and any small gaps can easily be repaired with bamboo thorns. The date palm (*Phœnix*) is also very good, as its armed leaves present a formidable obstacle to the intrusion of stray cattle. It will not, however, grow well everywhere. A living bamboo fence is also good, but not equal to those previously mentioned.

The Mexican Agave, again, makes a fine fence; but wild pigs are fond of the immature leaves, and destroy the whole plant to get at them. This was my experience in the Walliar Reserve.

A nursery must be formed near water, and beds made and planted-up with seeds of the best fuel-trees adapted to the soil of the Reserve. Vermin (rats) can be kept from the young plants by strewing pods of cowhage (*Mucuna pruriens*) round the stems of the seedlings. All perfectly open or bare spaces should be pitted 6′ × 6′, some being planted entirely with one single description of tree, whilst others should contain a mixture in order to determine which are the varieties that succeed best on the particular soil or soils of your block. In planting out, it will be necessary to remember that Casuarina succeeds best in a sandy soil, and *Acacia Arabica* in black cotton, and do not plant the Casuarina in the clay, and the babool in the sand.

On the Western Coast, at Mangalore, Casuarina does not thrive well in sand, even when water is only 4′ or 5′ below the surface, the growth being slow.

Your block being subdivided into smaller blocks of, say, fifty acres each, you can fell each over when they reach maturity, which will depend on the nature of the species growing in each block and the soil. As each compartment is felled, it can be either treated as coppice or replanted,—the former system being the best for such kinds as shoot freely from the stool, and the latter for those that do not.

The average outturn per acre for a mixed plantation will be about the same as in the case of the Australian wattle for the first crop; but the succeeding crops will bear no comparison with the sucker crop of Australian acacia that invariably succeeds a clean felling.

The following balance sheet will show the result of working a block of 500 acres for 12 years and 6 months. Assuming that you have had to pay such a price for the land, that any little profit realised by the felling and disposal of the timber or fuel already growing on it, just recoups you for the outlay you have incurred.

You may then expect to realise a profit, at the end of the eighth year on the first of your planted-up blocks; and supposing that you have felled and planted each block at intervals of 6 months, each compartment will be fit to fell just 6 months later than the one last cleared, and the last will be cleared 12 years and 6 months after the first was planted-up.

Of course the energetic fuel-planter may be more rapid in his rotations, and his returns will be proportionate.

By the end of the eighth year, the trees will average, if planted on fairly good soil, 10 inches in diameter at least, and weigh 300 lbs. a piece. It will take 8 such trees to produce a ton of firewood, and if they are planted 6 feet × 6 feet the acre of 1,200 trees will produce 150 tons at 8 rupees a ton = 1,200 rupees. Felling and lopping charges at 3 annas per tree will cost 225 rupees.

	RS.
Carting 150 tons at 1-8 per ton	225
Supervision and sundries, say	20

Then for 12½ years the profit on the whole 500-acre Block will be—

Expenditure.	RS.	*Receipts.*	RS.
750,000 plants at Rs. 5 per 1,000	3,750	By sale of 75,000 tons of Fuel at 8 rupees per ton.	6,00,000
Pitting 600,000 18-in. cube pits at 12 as. per 100 ...	4,500	Deduct charges	2,96,200
Shading and watering ... } Planting 500 acres ... }	2,000	Net profit ...	3,03,800
* Shading and watering at 30 rupees per acre ...	15,000		
2 Watchmen at 100 rupees a year each	2,500		
Quit-rent at 1 rupee per acre for 12½ years ...	6,250		
Total ...	34,000		
Simple interest at 10 per cent. for 8 years	27,200		
Felling and lopping 500 acres of Fuel at 225 rupees per acre	1,12,500		
Carting 75,000 tons at 1-8 per ton	1,12,500		
Supervision and sundries...	10,000		
Total ...	2,96,200		

Final Remarks :—It is difficult at present to fix the exact amount of calorific power of the various species of Indian trees. It may be taken for granted, however, that the denser and harder the wood, the higher the amount of calorific power it possesses. Resinous woods, and such as are of an oily nature, *e.g.*, teak, satinwood, sandal, blackwood, &c., burn with a fierce flame, but throw out dense

* Till plants are established.

volumes of pungent smoke, which more or less unfit them for fuel. Hard woods like tamarind, acha,* acacias, *Arabica*, *Sundra*, &c., burn with a fine clear flame and produce excellent charcoal. The manufacture of charcoal for iron smelting, forges, &c., may be profitably carried on, in connection with a Fuel Plantation; but this article is so light that it will bear carriage greater distance than fuel, and pay, and can therefore in many instances be more cheaply produced in Natural Forests, where the manufacture of this article is permitted to be carried on by Government or private individuals.

It is hardly within the scope of this article to describe minutely the manufacture of charcoal; suffice it to say, that it should never be made by the clumsy and wasteful native method of digging a pit, &c. The work should be conducted on scientific principles. The admission of air being carefully regulated as combustion proceeds, at the right moment it is totally excluded, the whole of the wood having been carbonised to the very core of each billet. The fire is extinguished from want of air, and when the charcoal is cold, it is collected, and ready for sale.

And now, a word or two about the tap-root. It is very necessary to a young plant, indeed, in some species, indispensable. It is the pump by which the young plant sucks up nourishment and moisture from often great depths. It is only necessary to examine the tap-root of the palmyra (*Borassus Flabelliformis*) seedling. It looks like a carrot, with a very long tail, and grows straight out of the nut without any appearance of foliage. It is not till long afterwards that the primary leaf appears. How unlike the cocoanut, where the leaf first appears out of the eye of the nut, the rootlets running in a fibrous network into the husk and over the shell of the nut! Why this difference? Because the cocoanut generally and naturally grows on the seashore, or the banks of tidal creeks; the nuts consequently, usually fall into the water, and drifting to the shore, speedily take

---

* *Hardwickia binata.*

root and grow. Far otherwise is it with the palmyra which grows often in the sandiest and most unprofitable looking ground. The seeds when moistened by the rains, drive their tap-roots deep into the soil, otherwise they could not possibly survive through the trying hot weather which follows. The tap-root is, therefore, a provision of nature, to enable the young plant to get into a region of moisture sufficient to enable it to pull through one dry season. The lateral roots are the ones that mainly supply the plant with food.

Pull up a young tamarind 4 feet high, it often has a tap-root 2 feet long! It is better to plant such seeds *in situ;* they do not bear transplanting well, or any docking of the tap-root.

You may have the required elevation, soil, and aspect, and yet fail in making your Fuel Plantation thrive, if you neglect paying attention to the amount of rainfall.

As an instance of this, I may cite the case of a few plants of *Acacia Dealbata* and *Eucalyptus Globulus* that were planted by Mr. Breeks in a sholah in the Khoondahs, beyond a place called Bhangy Tappal.

They could not have been planted in a better situation as far as appearances went, but when I visited them in 1879, I never saw anything more miserable than the growth they had made. The Acacias were only 3 feet high, and the *E. Globulus* only 7 feet! The excessive rainfall of this region, where over 300 inches fall during the monsoon, had been too much for them. I have only said a few words about the enemies that fuel-producing trees have. These may be classed as insect, animal, and vegetable.

In the earlier stages, insects may be accounted the most troublesome. Legions of ants devour some kinds of seed, when it is collected and put out to dry, and other legions carry it off, and bury it in their burrows the moment it is sown. If you put it away carelessly when you have collected it, you will discover to your cost that an army of weevils are in possession, and by drilling it full of holes, have rendered it worthless. All seeds should be kept in bottles carefully corked, and sealed up. Care should be taken that it is thoroughly *dry* before it is put into the bottles or it will get mouldy. After your seed has been planted, you will very likely find that a good deal has been dug up and eaten by field rats, &c., during the night, if it happens to suit their taste.

No sooner has the seed sprouted, than you find you have a fresh set of enemies to contend with, the larva of beetles, and of moths, to say nothing of mole-crickets, and the larvæ of certain butterflies, which look on the foliage as their special property. The first two burrow underground and only come up to feed at night. The young plants will be found to have been cut down at the base by the powerful nippers of these grubs, and often, row after row will be destroyed, and scarcely a plant eaten. The only remedy for this is to search for the depredator and destroy him. A tiny burrow will be seen where the larva has entered, after his night's work, generally near the stem of the last plant cut over, and if the ground is carefully turned up with a pointed stick, the insect will be found not far off. Mole-crickets cut down plants in the same way at night. They can be caught by placing a lantern at night where they are troublesome with a pit 14 × 15 inches in which a tin pot with a little oil at the bottom has been placed. The crickets attracted by the light, fall in, and get drowned. Sometimes the roots of seedlings are attacked by worms and other insect foes. A mixture of salt, lime, and powdered tobacco sprinkled round the base of plants so afflicted, will be found an excellent remedy, as the whole of this is dissolved by the water applied to the plant, and wash down to the roots, which it does not injure. If rats are found troublesome, apply the pods of the cowhage creeper (*Mucuna pruriens*) to the base of the plants. Not a rat will go near them, as the velvety prickles which thickly coat the pod, cause an intolerable itching if touched,—this must be remembered by the person applying the pods, or he will get the bristles into his own hands and suffer severely. There are two species in Southern India,—one with deep, orange bristles set in parallel rows, and the other of an olive green, thickly covered with spines. The cowhage, or cowitch as it is popularly called, is known in Tamil as *Poonay Poodkoo Kodie*. If your nursery is situated low down near water, you may be troubled with land crabs. These are very troublesome, clearing a whole bed of *every* plant in a single night. I have poured a gallon of a mixture of quicklime and urine down their holes every day for a week; but found that it made not the slightest impression on them. The fruit of *Emblica Officinalis*, known as *Nellikai* in Tamil, is excellent. The round little fruit can be rolled like marbles into the crab holes—ten or twenty into a hole. They decay in the water at the bottom of the burrow, and make it foul, and unfit for the crabs,—it is even said to kill them; but I have no proof of this.

When the young plants in your plantation are a few feet high, the stem is often bored out, by the larva of beetles of various species. The watcher in charge should go round with a bit of soft copper wire 2 feet long and one-tenth of an inch in diameter, and after removing the excrement of the insect which it cunningly felts together with silk, and uses as a screen to hide the entrance to its tunnel, probe the hole with the wire, which from its softness will follow the curve upwards or downwards as the case may be. The point of the wire will generally pass through the insect, if he is at home, and kill him—and this can be ascertained by examining the point of the wire when it is extracted, when it will be found to be wet, and covered with portions of the slain insect.

If, however, in addition to boring the tree, the larva has girdled it as well—the best plan is to coppice it below the limit of the tunnel, and cut the top of the severed stool neatly into a cone. The fuel-planter has still a multitude of enemies to deal with, for as the trees grow up, some species are almost entirely destroyed, or, at all events, have their growth greatly retarded by various species of *Loran-*

thus, which, frugiverous birds and bats plant for him, on the boughs of his trees. *Acacia Melanoxylon* is particularly liable to be injured in this way,—the little Nílgiri Flower Pecker, *Dicæum Concolor*, being the culprit usually, who distributes the seeds. All species of Loranthus are the Leeches of the Vegetable Kingdom, and suck the sap out of every plant, they thrust their cruel roots into. The only remedy is to cut them out as they appear—if the trees are not too high. Unless a plantation is meant to be a mixed one of fuel and timber, it is not worth while bothering about Loranthus.

Hares do no damage to young fuel-plantations in India. Deer, Sambur, occasionally rub their horns against a tree here and there, and scrape off a little bark, but this is all.

Domestic cattle, when they break in, play the very mischief, breaking down trees with their horns, barking them, and trampling the young seedings in nurseries to death. Goats eat nearly everything, and will speedily put an end to a fuel-plantation, if they are sufficiently numerous, and get in very often.

In the plains the Casuarina seed should be collected in April. If removed much later, 50 per cent. of the cones will have cast their seeds. In the Wynaad, seed can be collected from June till December! In the nursery beds, if you wish to force your young plants of this species on, a compost 34 inches deep should be made. This, of course, will add considerably to the cost of the plants, but it is a decided advantage if you are late in the season. The compost should be made as follows:—

30 per cent. of rich mould or humus.
20 per cent. of sand or brick-dust.
30 per cent. of two years' old cattle-manure.
20 per cent. of saw-dust—not teak.

If the soil is porous, and water far from the surface, the tap-root should not be shortened, unless it is over 18 inches in length, when the tap-root *must* be cut if your pit is 18 inches cube, or be doubled up. If the season is a hot one, the beds in the nursery ought to be carefully shaded. Forked uprights 7 feet high should be put into the ground 8 feet apart and a pandal covered with a bamboo or *woday coochy* (*Bheesa Travancorica*) or any of the lesser bamboos tatty constructed. This tempers the noon-day heat, and provides a sufficiency of light. The Casuarina seed is very light, and will not bear being too thickly covered with mould, one-eighth of an inch is sufficient, just enough to prevent its being blown away by wind. Any heavy rush of water, such as that from a watering pot, will drown the seed and wash it to the surface. What I have already said about the fine spray, from a garden engine, must be remembered. If the beds are made of compost, no percolation worth anything will take place, if the channel system of watering is adopted, as described earlier. If the soil is constantly kept damp, and this is a *sine qua non*, the seeds will germinate in from ten days to a fortnight. If water is close to the surface of your soil, pursue the method pointed out for *E. Globulus* of transplanting once, previous to planting out. The Casuarina ought to have its tap-root cut, this is to be done, when it is 3—4 inches high to make it produce lateral roots. No plant should be put out less than 9 inches high, and not over 1½ feet. Plants can be reared in bamboo pots, where these are large, abundant and cheap. The joint should be 2 inches from the bottom of the pot, to allow of drainage, and should have a few pieces of broken brick, or tile, placed over a hole ½ inch in diameter drilled through the diaphragm, also for that purpose. The mouth of the pot should be the larger end of the bamboo joint. With bamboo pots, the plants can be put down, pot and all, as whiteants quickly eat up the bamboo, and free the roots, and if this does not happen, the bamboo rots from combined heat and moisture, and the roots pass through the sides; the tap-root generally makes its way through the bottom of the pot *at once*, when the bamboo is put into the ground.

With Eucalyptus the planter will find it necessary to trim the tree to a mere tuft of leaves at the top, just before the monsoon gales commence. If this is not done, the seedling will get wind-wrung at the base, or even be completely uprooted, or bent on one side. In Cuddapah, Casuarinas have been established at a cost of less than 2½ annas per tree, but this may be taken as under the mark.

I have given a list of a few of the best fuel producing trees, and likewise of a few that should not be planted; but, as the number of these last is legion, it is better that the fuel-planter should only plant those that have been already *proved* a success, and not try any rash experiments *on a large scale*, with new species.

CHAPTER XIII.

HUMUS AND THE DEFERTILIZATION OF FOREST SOILS, &c., IN INDIA.

Nature of Forests. I WILL begin by dividing the forests of India into three broad classes:—

(1) The deciduous forests;
(2) The tropical evergreen forests;
(3) The alpine shola forests.

The first class may again be subdivided into two divisions:—

(*a*) Heavy deciduous forests where no grass grows;
(*b*) Open deciduous forest in which there is a rank growth of coarse grass.

In (*a*) we find a little humus in hollows; but on all slopes, there is an utter absence of it. The soil is usually a deep chocolate brown on the surface; but lower down the subsoil is yellow. Forest fires annually burn the thick layer of leaves that carpet the ground in January or February; but such fires burn slowly and with little flame. In the (*b*) class of forests, fires annually rage, sweeping everything clean before them and doing enormous damage.

In such forests in the Wynaad, the soil is a rich black loam; but elsewhere, where the soil is poor, by nature, and the forest scanty, it may be red, brown or other colours and either stony, gravelly, or rocky, as the case may be.

In class (2) tropical evergreen forests, fire, as a rule, never enters; an abundance of leaves are shed annually on the ground; and yet, strange to say, no humus worth speaking of is to be seen except in hollows, and in the monsoon, the greater portion of the shed leaves will be found to have disappeared. The soil, however, is generally rich, and of a dark-brown or black color. In the 3rd class—the alpine shola forests—the ground will be found covered to a great depth, with the finest humus—the forester's ideal covering for the surface of the soil of his forest. The covering which prevents wash, absorbs the rainfall, and retards evaporation. To have the soil of his deciduous forests covered with, a thick layer of humus is a dream of the Indian forester's; but a dream it will continue to be and nothing else, as I purpose proving further on.

In Southern India *real* humus does not exist below 4,000 feet. The higher you go above it, the more humus you find; but above 6,000 feet, the depth of humus is constant.

Let us enter a shola, say on the Neilgherries, and proceed to examine the surface soil. First we remove a dense covering of leaves, some bright orange and red and quite pliable that have but just fallen, others crisp and yellow that have been there for weeks, and others again, in the layer below that have lain there for months, leaves in which the skeleton is wholly or partly exposed. Then below that layer again, we find a multitude of brittle bits of twigs, the shells of berries and fruit, black with age, seeds that have been bored by insects or emptied by rats and squirrels, particles of decayed leaves, the crumbled cases of empty shells and remnants of insects, long since dead and gone, mixed up with the excretæ of a host of earthworms. Below this last stratum, we find a layer of soil, in which it is barely possible to distinguish the fine particles of vegetable origin that almost entirely compose it. Now, why should there be this difference between the forests of this class and the preceding ones? The casual observer is easily able to account for the want of humus in deciduous forests. It is all burnt up annually he says, how then can there be humus? No doubt forest fires burn up every particle of dry vegetable matter they can get at; but if a forest at a low elevation were protected from fire for a century, there would still be no humus!

Annually the trees of deciduous forests shed countless millions of leaves on the surface on which they grow. Their dead branches and trunks fall, and rot where they lie (if not burnt up) and yet there is no humus! Countless hosts of insects are at work carefully collecting and burying every particle of vegetable matter, that is devoid of life. Every leaf and twig that falls is instantly covered with a layer of earth by the teeming millions of white ants (*Termes*) that inhabit all tropical countries, and carried piecemeal deep into the earth. Every tree that dies or falls is bored into and reduced to powder by other countless hosts of longicorn and other beetles, everything being subsequently buried by the termites in their galleries from two to twelve feet underground. In course of time other myriads of earthworms devour the vegetable substances thus hidden, with quantities of the finer particles of the soil, which they throw up to the surface of the soil in the shape of what is known as worm "castings."

Thus the leaf mould is not lost but only hidden from sight, to reappear in a different form on the surface of the soil.

But in the deciduous forests the fall of leaves is so very sudden that the white ants have but little time to collect the harvest before the forest fires devour it. Instead therefore of the leaves, twigs and trunks returning to the soil, what was taken from it for their formatiom, they are burnt to ashes which the winds of heaven and April storms carry far and wide. In the course of centuries and centuries, the soil of deciduous grass forests becomes mixed with the fine particles of charred grass, which sometimes lie to the depth of an inch or so on the surface after a forest fire. These are swallowed with atoms of earth and grass by earthworms, and thus thoroughly mixed with the soil, which in this manner obtains its dark colour.

In the heavy evergreen tropical forests, on the other hand, forest fires never (or very seldom) enter. The legions of earthworms that inhabit the soils of such forests devour and throw up to the surface almost pure vegetable humus, and this operation being continually carried on for ages, gradually covers stones, and gravel often to a great depth, with a rich and finely comminuted vegetable soil.

We are little aware what important services are being rendered to us by such despised insects as white ants, and earthworms; were it not for the former, *all* vegetable substances would be burnt up in deciduous forests and wasted, and the soil gradually but surely impoverished; and were it not for the latter, the substances buried by the former would not be returned to the surface of the soil, and thus brought within reach of surface rooting plants, nor would soils—barren and gravelly or stoney on the surface be coated with a rich mould which the tender radicles of the fallen seeds of forest trees find no difficulty in penetrating and absorbing food from.

Not only do white ants improve the soil by burying vegetable substances in it, but by continually carrying to the surface the finer particles of the soil from great depths, both for the construction of their tumuli and for purposes of protection from their enemies, for they coat everything they attack with a thin layer of fine earth, before gnawing it away, they perform for us some of the services of the earthworm in burying gravel and stones.

Not only are forests affected by these two great classes of insects, but pasturages are improved by the earthworm, which annually coats the surface of the soil, in some places, to a depth of nearly two inches, with its castings.

Koomaree Cultivation.

Of all varieties of cultivation carried on in the world, this is the most pernicious. It is variously known in India, under the names of Koomaree, Tuckle, Ponnam, Kothkad, &c., and in Burma as Toungya.

The system on which it is practised is as follows: A tract of virgin forest is selected, felled in November or December and burnt in March or April. Paddy or millet (*Eleusine Coracana*) is sown when the first showers fall on the ashes of the clearing the ground in some districts being scratched up by a stick or small hoe. With the grain are sown the seeds of cucumbers, pumpkins and Indian corn (*Zea Mays*). When the crop has been reaped, the clearing is abandoned, to be recultivated after a lapse of years, amounting from six to twenty-five according to the area of forest at the disposal of the aboriginal tribe who practise this method of cultivation.

In Wynaad, the Coorchas, Kaders, Moopahs, Jain Curumbers, Bett Curumbers, Naikas; in Palghat the Mulcers; on the Anamallays the Puliars, Kaders, Moodugas, &c.; in Coimbatore the Irulars, Sholagars and Kosuvas; in Kurnool, Cuddapah, &c., the Chentsuas and Yenadies; and in Burma the Karens are almost entirely dependant on this system of cultivation for a living.

The process to which the soil of a forest 'Tuckled' is subjected is this:—

The accumulated vegetable growth and humus of years is burnt to ashes in February. The heavy thunder-storms of April and May wash the lighter particles into streams and rivers by which they are carried away to the sea and lost.

The heavy rains of the southwest monsoon complete the mischief.

At the end of from ten to fifteen years the soil is once again covered with a growth of low forest—nature's effort to repair the mischief done. But just at this period the junglewallah thinks it about time he had a second crop off the same plot. So he fells and burns it once more, and again with the advent of the monsoon, the surface soil travels to the sea.

The roots of giant forest trees penetrate the soil to great depths and bring up to the surface the elements of plant-life there found. The koomaree cultivator therefore not only exhausts the soil on the surface but to great depths below. The result is that each successive crop of trees is not as vigorous as the one preceding. Until in course of time trees refuse to grow at all, and a scrubby growth of thorns takes its place. If, especially on steep declivities, the thorns are also "Tuckled," finally everything will cease to grow, and disastrous landslips take place. In fields under the plough, especially where high cultivation is practised, it is easy enough to restore the fertility of lands exhausted by cereals or root crops, by turning up the sub-soil, and heavy manuring; but how is it possible to restore the fertility of a soil required for the growth of trees where every particle of vegetable food has been abstracted by the roots of successive growths of trees for generations and generations, and then finally removed entirely from the surface of the soil by the united action of rain and floods?

It will be seen from this of what vital importance it is to the well-being of the country that this system of cultivation especially on steep slopes should be put an entire stop to.

Our mountain chains especially, consist almost entirely of a skeleton of solid rock—gneiss, covered in many instances with but a thin coating of soil, derived from the decomposition of the felspar in it. Many portions of the Western Ghâts, the Chenat Nair (Palghat) Forests for instance, have barely an average coating of twenty feet of soil on them and where the practice of koomaree cultivation is steadily carried on, it is not difficult to predict how long it will take for the bare rock to appear in all its naked deformity. Unfortunately, very large areas of the Ghat Forest belong to private proprietors, whose only thought is to cut them to pieces, and realise every farthing that can be wrung from them as soon as possible. The only thing that has protected them so far has been the large numbers of inferior trees which do not repay the cost of removal. Koomaree cultivation, however, if it extends much, will finally effect this, except on the very steepest ridges.

Forest fires, rainfall and the action of animals.

I have explained the manner in which earthworms improve the soil and cover up stones and gravel by their castings. These castings are hard and clayey in nature, and not easily dissolved by rainfall, however heavy. In grass lands which are fired annually by village herdsmen, these nodules of insect-formed clay are partly calcined by the action of fire and then fully exposed to the united action of sun and rain, which tends to pulverise them. When the young grass has sprouted, large herds of cattle are driven up from the plains to graze on the tender and succulent green shoots. They trample on and reduce the clay nodules to dust. Heavy storms follow in April and May, and the finely pulverised soil is washed down the steep slopes into streams and lost. Cattle also by continually treading on the humus and worm-castings in forests trample the soil (where level) into a hard compact mass, which the delicate radicles of seeds cannot penetrate. Reproduction is, therefore, seriously interfered with.

Restoration of exhausted soils.

The only possible way in which soils exhausted by koomaree cultivation can be restored is to put an entire stop to it. If the mischief has proceeded so far that reboisement is necessary it should be taken in hand at once, and the areas requiring it planted up with such descriptions of trees as suit the climate and locality, and are likely to bind the soil with their roots. For high elevations the *Acacia dealbata* answers excellently for this purpose. Some species of ficus are also very good, especially those that throw out an abundance of ærial roots such are suited for low elevations. It may be contended that the aboriginal tribes have practised the koomaree system of cultivation from time immemorial—that it is impossible to put a stop to it. There is considerable truth in this; but the word impossible in this instance should form no part of the Indian Forester's Vocabulary. To *suppress* the practice will take years and years. The aboriginal tribes must be found some other means of employment. They must be civilised. Lands must be set apart for them and *permanent* villages built. They must be encouraged to plant fruit trees and grow other crops than those they have been accustomed to. They must be taught trades and stimulated to practise such as they engage in at present, *e.g.*, the manufacture of pottery, of basket-work and the art of the blacksmith. Congenial employment must be found for them by the Forest Department, such as timber squaring, the collection of forest produce, &c., and deserving men should be employed as watchers, elephant-drivers and maistries. They can be made of the greatest service to the Forest Department or the reverse, as they happen to be treated; at present, they are aliens and outcastes, swindled by everybody and oppressed by every peon and policeman in the country. How can the Curumber be expected to rise in the scale of civilization when he dare not possess property? If he invests in a few fowls, sheep, or goats, the first peon who happens to see them will at once appropriate them to his own use. If he grows vegetables, they too will be stolen from him and the unfortunate owner most probably be made to carry them to the house of his despoiler. Dare the wretched man complain—he is kicked and beaten. This picture is not over-coloured in any way. It is what actually occurs in every forest and almost every day.

Tracts of forests that have been much "Tuckled" must be closed and carefully conserved for perhaps centuries before they can be expected to recover from the mischief done to them.

Grass lands will have to be fire-traced, and no cattle permitted to graze over them when recently burnt. When, however, the monsoon has restored the thick carpet of grass, that should naturally cover them, cattle can do but little harm. The grazing of cattle, as already pointed out on steep slopes, but recently burnt, is likely to cause damage and loss of much valuable surface soil.

The operations of the coffee planter on steep slopes are often so carelessly carried on that as much or more damage is done by him in a shorter space of time than even by the koomaree cultivator.

Many a planter opens up a much larger area than he has the capital to cultivate properly. The steepest slopes and ridges are recklessly denuded. The soil is continually and diligently dug up and pulverised just at the time of heaviest rainfall and may be seen during a heavy storm, hurrying in a coffee-coloured torrent to the sea. In ten years, he undoes the work of centuries, and finally abandons the impoverished soil covered with a wretched growth of thorns and brambles. On such steep slopes landslips may be confidently expected, and must in the nature of things occur.

Having ruined one block of valuable forests, he hastens to ruin another. A marked contrast to the careful and scientific planter who having selected land with a gentle slope works on a rational method, saves his soil in catch-drains or soil-pits and manures liberally, returning to the soil a fair equivalent of what he has taken from it. It is said that the man who makes two blades of grass grow where only one grew before is a benefactor to mankind; but he who destroys a valuable forest and leaves it a wilderness of thorns and weeds cannot be considered such. The ignorant and careless planter not only ruins the land actually cultivated by him, but frequently damages the surrounding forest as well by allowing the fire from his felling to extend into it by which number of trees are scorched and killed and others seriously injured. The felling is frequently so situated that wind enters and uproots the trees all round near its edge, and these with those already fallen, furnish the materials for a fire that still further damages the forest.

CHAPTER XIV.

ON FOREST PRODUCTS.

THE forests of Malabar are some of the finest in the Presidency. They cover an enormous area of the district. The genera and species of trees, &c., comprised in the Flora are numerous, and varied, and the economic products yielded by them, equally so.

In the enumeration of these products and the method of their collection, I will classify them in the following order:—

(1) Gums, resins and oleo-resins.
(2) Oils, essential and fixed.
(3) Tan barks and dyes.
(4) Fibres, and paper materials.
(5) Spices, drugs and medicinal roots.
(6) Edible fruits, roots, &c.
(7) Sundry products.

Acacia Arabica.—This tree occurs sparingly in the Palghât Taluq of the district. Gum exudes from fissures in the bark, or knife cuts, purposely or accidentally made, in the dry weather. It is of excellent quality, of a pale straw or yellowish red colour, and is occasionally eaten by children. The amount produced in the district is so small as to be hardly worth mentioning.

Acacia Sundra found in the Walayar reserves; but does not extend further west or south; produces a fair catechu. I have not, however, known it manufactured in the district.

Adenanthéra pavonina yields a clear gum, not collected.

Aegle Marmelos yields a poor brown gum in round nodules.

Ailanthus Malabarica found in the Anamallays; yields a brownish coloured plastic resin known as *Muttipâl.* It is extensively burnt as incense by the natives. The Mulcers,

Khaders, Puliars and other jungle tribes search the forests for it in the dry weather, and barter it for rice, chillies, cloth, &c., to the bazaar men, who yearly travel into the forest to the "*pathies*" or villages of the aboriginal tribes to obtain it and other forest products.

Albizzia Lebbek yields a clear gum copiously, if the bark is cut or injured in the dry weather.

Albizzia Odorattissima.—The gum of this tree is poor in quality, and dark in colour. It is only obtainable in the dry weather, by hacking the trunk of a tree with a knife.

Alstonia Scholaris.—A very handsome evergreen tree found everywhere in the district, from the sea-level to nearly 3,000 feet in the Wynaad. An abundance of milky sap flows out of the bark when cut, which has some of the qualities of caoutchouc about it; but is sticky, and more fit for bird-lime. Some of these trees in the evergreen forests of the Chenat Nair forests are over thirty feet in circumference.

Anacardium occidentale.—The cashew-nut has taken kindly to the west coast where it has found a congenial soil, and climate, and spread everywhere; it produces an excellent gum, which is used by book-binders as a protection against cockroaches and other insects.

Anogeissus latifolia occurs throughout Malabar up to 2,500 feet elevation. Produces an abundance of excellent clear gum, if the bark is injured. It is not, however, collected in the district.

Areca Catechu—Cultivated. The seeds of the wild species contain a large percentage of tannin, and catechu could no doubt be extracted from them. The aboriginal tribes, however, only chew the nuts with wild betel (*Chavica betel*) leaves, and lime made from the shells of fresh water snails.

Artocarpus integrifolia—The jack tree. Common in the forests of the Western Ghâts; produces an abundance of milky sap which on exposure coagulates. It is occasionally used as bird-lime, when combined with the milky sap of various species of ficus, the oil made from the seeds of *Schleichera trijuga, &c.* The seeds of the wild jack are also roasted and eaten by aboriginal tribes, containing a large percentage of farinaceous matter, as, they do, they are considered very wholesome.

Artocarpus hirsuta.—The Iynee or Angelly, a magnificent tree found throughout the district; produces an abundance of milky sap, which dries into a dark-coloured mass. The seeds are eaten.

Bassia latifolia.—Common in the Palghat Taluq, yields an abundance of milky sap of no particular value. The seeds and flowers are valuable. The former for the large percentage of excellent oil it contains, and the latter for the manufacture of arrack.

Bauhinias Sp.—All the Bauhinias yield gum none of which is ever collected in the district.

Bombax Malabaricum.—A very common tree everywhere, yields the dark, dirty-coloured gum like Tragacanth of little value. The natives use it medicinally.

Butea frondosa.—Common everywhere, from the sea-level to 2,500 feet (Wynaad) yields a lovely clear astringent gum, very like gum Kino, might be used for tanning leather and staining wood. It is used medicinally by the natives; but is not collected in any quantity.

Callophyllum Augustifolium.—A handsome evergreen tree, abundant in the Ghât forests, produces a clear greenish resin, which never hardens. It is not collected.

Calatropis gigantea.—Common in the Palghat Taluq; yields a poor description of gutta. The milky sap is valued by the natives and used medicinally. The bark yields a very strong and silky fibre used for fishing-lines.

Canarium Strictum.—A gigantic tree of the Western Ghâts. The Coorchias of Wynaad obtain the resin which it produces in abundance, by lighting a fire at the base of the tree on the side towards which it is inclined. When the bark has been well charred, the resin begins to exude and huge stalactitic masses are formed which are collected five or six months after the charring of the bark has taken place. The market price at Calicut varies from one anna six pies to two annas per lb. It is almost black in appearance with a vitreous fracture; but if held up to the light is found to be translucent and of a golden-red tint. It is principally used for sealing bottles, jars, &c. I have found that in combination with Kerosene oil, this resin forms an excellent, though slow drying varnish, which however will not stand exposure to damp or wet.

Careya arborea yields a clear gum which is not collected. The bark also yields an excellent fibre, and the leaves are the favorite food of the Tassa silk worm (Antheræa paphia). The apple-like fruit of this tree is eagerly devoured by cattle.

Cathartocarpus (Cassia) Fistula yields a reddish astringent gum used medicinally. The bark is used for tanning leather, and the black treacly substance found adhering to the divisions between the seeds in the long brown pods is used medicinally as a cathartic.

Cedrela toona yields a gum resin not collected in the district.

Chloroxylon Swietenia.—The satin wood is only found near Walayar and is scarce there. It yields a clear pale gum. The sawdust of the heartwood is very fragrant and smells like new ginger bread. It is very unctuous to the feel, and a good wood oil could doubtless be extracted from it.

Cryptostegia grandiflora yields a splendid quality of Caoutchouc far superior to the Ceara (*Manihot Glazovii*) rubber. The work of collecting the sap from the ends of the young shoots is, however, very tedious, and the cultivation of this climber is on that account not likely to pay. The caoutchouc is easily separated from the sap, by the addition of a small quantity of spirits, and by heating the sap gently over a charcoal fire. The Cryptostegia is only cultivated in gardens in the district.

Diospyros Embryopteris, found from the sea coast up to 2,500 feet elevation (Wynaad). This tree affects the neighbourhood of streams as a rule. The fruit contains a large quantity of very clear liquid gum which is exceedingly astringent. This gum is used for tanning fishing-lines, nets, &c., and in colouring and glazing the slices of areca nuts which are sold in the bazaars.

Erythrina Indica.—Common throughout Malabar, both cultivated and wild; yields a poor gum of a dark colour.

Euphorbia Nivulia yields a copious supply of milky sap of poisonous odour. On congelation, it produces a hard somewhat brittle, yellow gum which partially melts when thrown into hot water. This Euphorbia is very common on the low laterite hills near Calicut.

Euphorbia Pulcherima.—This shrub is cultivated in gardens for its lovely scarlet bracts. The milky sap produces, when dried, a darkish gum.

Ficus Elastica.—This fig has only recently been introduced into Malabar, and is growing well in the Manantoddy Botanical Garden. The India rubber produced by it, is too well known to need description.

Ficus religiosa.—The peepul is a common tree throughout the district. Its milky sap hardens into an inferior Gutta Percha.

Garcinia pictoria (Morella).—A common tree on the Western Ghât where it grows in the heavy evergreen forests at an elevation of from 1,000 to 2,500 feet. This species produces the true gamboge of commerce; but it seems to be greatly neglected. I have found on prodding the bark with an awl that a small mass of excellent gamboge appears of about the size of a pea. If the bark is cut, tears of gamboge collect along the edges of the bark, where cut, and dry. The easiest way of extracting the gamboge is to scrape the bark carefully, so as to remove all particles of dead bark, moss, and other impurities. The bark is then peeled off the trunk, and pounded in a mortar. The whole of the colouring matter is extracted by six or eight hours of boiling. The extract thus obtained is to be inspissated over a charcoal fire, and when the liquid portions have been sufficiently evaporated, the residue may be sun-dried, after being moulded in blocks. The product thus obtained is inferior to the natural exudation, having a greenish tinge. Gamboge is used medicinally, and in the arts as a paint. There are other species of gamboge-producing trees (*Garcinias*) in the shola forests of the district; but the gamboge produced by them is, on the whole, inferior to that from this species. *G. Wightii* and *G. Travancorica*; both produce very fair gamboge.

Isonandra Wightiana.—This magnificent evergreen tree produces copiously a thick milky sap which hardens into a kind of Gutta Percha. Commercially it has at present no value.

Lagerstroemia Microcarpa yields sparingly a gum resin, of no particular value.

L. Flos Reginæ.—This species also yields a gum resin very similar to the above.

Macaranga tomentosa.—Evergreen forests. Yields in small quantities a medicinal gum.

Melia Azadarachta yields freely and in large quantities a clear gum, which is used medicinally in India.

Moringa pteriggosperma cultivated in Malabar, yields a dark-coloured gum used medicinally, otherwise of no value.

Odina Wodier yields quantities of a bright clear gum, which is used in calico-printing, &c.

Poinciana regia yields gum of a pale straw colour in small quantities.

Pterocarpus marsupium.—A valuable timber tree of the deciduous forests, yields an abundance of ruby-coloured sap which hardens, and breaks up into small garnet-coloured grains. This gum resin is exceedingly astringent and is used medicinally and to stain wood. The *Myristica Malabarica* also yields an abundance of kino.

Sapindus detergens occurs in Palghat; yields a gum. The seeds are collected, the epicarp being used as a substitute for soap.

Semecarpus Anacardium.—A common tree. The bark, and seeds, produce a black substance, which is exceedingly poisonous to some people. I have obtained a black varnish from the seeds by roasting and squeezing them. The fumes are, however, during this process, exceedingly noxious, causing swellings and partial blindness. It is dangerous to stand under these trees at night or during rainy weather; for the drops from the leaves will produce swellings of the face and body.

The *Semecarpus Travancorica,* is equally dangerous.

Shorea laccifera occurs only in the Beni tract of the Wynaad forests. It yields an abundance of a fragrant resin known as "*Sambrani*" burnt as incense by the natives.

Spondias Mangifera yields a dark gum of poor quality.

Sponia orientalis.—Occasionally a little gum is to be obtained from this tree; but it is of little or no value. The bark yields a fibre.

Sterculia Villosa yields a gum of no value. The bark however yields excellent fibre, of which elephant drag ropes are made in Malabar.

Tectona grandis.—The wood of the Teak tree yields a tar, very similar to coal tar in appearance. It would be of value for tarring timber where white ants are abundant, and destructive, for they show a great dislike to the oil of Teakwood, and will not touch it as long as the oil remains in it.

Terminalia bellerica.—A lofty tree, of the deciduous forests, yields a quantity of clear gum which is not however collected.

Vateria Malabarica.—This species yield an abundance of a clear green resin known as "*Vellay kongilium*" by the natives, and is used by them as an incense. The bark of the tree is notched when the resin flows and gradually hardens. It makes an excellent varnish, if melted with spirits of Turpentine, and clear shell lac.

Xylia dolabriformis.—The Irul—a hard wooded timber tree of the lowlands of Malabar. The timber of this tree is exceedingly resinous, and a tar might be obtained from it. Another ironwood the *Mesua ferrea,* yields copiously both from the bark and green fruit, a semi-liquid resin of a strong odour.

Oils—Essential and Fixed.

Adenanthara pavonina.—The beautiful scarlet seeds of this tree produce an oil, which is not much used, as the trees are scarce.

Albizzia Lebbek.—The seeds of this tree contain a small quantity of oil which is used medicinally by the natives.

Aleurites moluccana—cultivated both in the Wynaad and the low country. It produces two crops of seeds in a year, and the seeds often lie for years on the ground before germinating. This tree is very quick in its growth and produces large crops. The nuts contain a large percentage of the finest oil. They are also edible, if kept for any length of time, but if eaten fresh, they are poisonous. This tree is well worthy of attention, and should be extensively propagated.

Ellettaria Cardamomum.—This is the most important forest product, yielded by the grand forests of Malabar. The outturn of cardamoms now in Malabar has fallen far short of what it used to be. The cultivation not having been attended to of late years. This, however, will soon be remedied; for the important reserved forests of Peria in Wynaad will shortly be leased out, and the cultivation of this valuable spice encouraged in every way. The crop ripens in October, and sells when cured for rates varying from Rs. 50 to Rs. 110 a tulâm = 32lbs. English. The seeds are principally used as spices and medicinally, and an essential oil is extracted from them by distillation which is used medicinally as a carminative, and for disguising the taste of nauseous drugs. For particulars regarding the cultivation of this spice, I refer the reader to Ludlow and Owen's pamphlets on the subject.

Anacardium occidentale.—Cashew-nuts are largely eaten roasted both by Europeans and Natives. They contain a large percentage of a clear, bland oil, which is far superior to olive oil, and might be used for oiling delicate machinery. The demand for the nuts is however so great that the oil is never likely to become a marketable product. The tree is abundant on the west coast, and self-sown seed comes up everywhere. The pericarp of the nut contains about 30 per cent. of a powerful caustic oil, that blisters where it touches the skin. This oil is used for polishing gunstocks. The pedicel of the seed is fleshy of a brilliant golden or pinkish red colour, very juicy; but slightly astringent. It is largely eaten by the natives in the hot weather. It however leaves an unpleasant acrid feeling behind in the throat.

Anamirta Cocculus.—The fruit of this climber is used to adulterate beer. The seeds contain a fatty oil.

Andropogon Muricatum.—Khus-khus grass grows wild, and is cultivated in Malabar. The roots are used for Khus-khus tatties in the hot weather. When distilled with water, a delicious essential oil is obtained, having the peculiar and fragrant odour of these grass roots when wet.

Andropogon Citratus.—Lemon grass grows plentifully on the slopes of the Western Ghâts everywhere. When distilled, it produces a fragrant essential oil which is used by perfumers.

Andropogon Nardus.—Citronelle grass is found wild in patches on the Western Ghâts. It is also cultivated. From 17lbs. of grass I distilled 1¾oz. of essential oil of a yellowish brown colour, exceedingly fragrant and closely resembling the odour of crushed Verbena leaves. It is largely used by perfumers and soap-makers at home. There are large distilleries devoted to the extraction of this oil in Ceylon.

Atalantia monophylla.—The leaves of this thorny plant yield an essential oil. The rind of the berries also contains it.

The Neilgherry Atalantia.—A thorny climber, contains an abundance of essential oil in its leaves and berries. I distilled a quantity of both, and found the odour to closely resemble that of essential oil of Citronelle.

Bassia latifolia.—The seeds of this large tree produce a quantity of fatty oil which is used to adulterate ghee. It is common in the Palghat Taluq. The seeds of the *Isonandras* also contain a large percentage of fatty oil. They are not however utilized.

Benincasa Cerifera.—This pumpkin is cultivated in our forests by the Curumbers, &c. The blue bloom on its surface can be scraped off and melted into a kind of vegetable wax. The natives, however, are ignorant of this. The seeds contain a mild pale oil as indeed do those of all species belonging to this order (*Cucurbitaceæ*).

Bombax Malabaricum.—The seeds of the silk cotton tree contains a large percentage of a thin colourless oil, which is not made any use of.

Buchanania latifolia.—The Cheroonjie nut grows on the confines of Mysore. The seeds are excellent eating, and contain a quantity of bland limpid oil. The seeds are in such demand however that the oil is never extracted.

Butea frondosa.—The seeds yield a medicinal oil.

Callophyllum Angustifolium.—The seeds of this tree yield a bright green oil of a peculiar odour; it is used for lamps. All the other species of *Callophyllum* also bear oil-producing seeds.

Carapa moluccensis yields a fatty oil by expression—used for burning in lamps.

Cerbera Odallum.—The poisonous mangoe-shaped fruits of this small tree yield an oil which is used for lamps.

Cinnamomum Zeylanicum.—The species and varieties of this tree in Malabar are innumerable. Their leaves contain an essential oil of a strong aromatic odour. The bark, when distilled, produces another fragrant essential oil, and the bark of the roots of many species contains camphor.

Croton tiglium.—The seeds of this species contain a large percentage of oil, which is used medicinally by natives, and others as a powerful purgative, and externally as a blister.

Cynometra ramiflora.—The *Irrupu*—yields from its seeds a medicinal oil.

Diospyros Embryopteris.—The seeds yield a pale-coloured oil, which is used medicinally by the natives.

Flaycourtia Raymontchi.—The seeds yield an oil.

Garcinia pictoria.—The fruit of the Gamboge tree is pickled by the natives, and a yellow fatty oil is expressed from the seeds known as Cocum butter. It is used medicinally, and for burning.

Melia Azidirachta.—Neem oil is extracted from the small yellow fruit of this tree. It is dark-yellow in colour, and possesses an unpleasant taste and smell. It is used medicinally, and for the cure of mange in dogs. Natives seem to have great faith in it. It is also used for burning; but produces a heavy and pungent smoke.

Mesua ferrea.—In addition to the resin with which the fruit is generally coated, the seeds contain a brownish oil, which is used medicinally and for burning.

Mimusops Elengi.—The seeds of this tree which is found in the Western Ghâts produce a medicinal oil.

Moringa pterygosperma.—The seeds of this tree produce a large quantity of oil which when clarified and freed from impurities is used by watch-makers and perfumers. It is an excellent oil for gun locks. The seed pods are, however, so extensively used when young as a vegetable that it is not surprising the oil cannot be obtained in larger quantities.

Myristica Malabarica.—This fine tree of the Ghât forests produces a nutmeg covered with a mace. The seed when pounded and boiled, throws up to the surface of the water an olive-green viscid resinous oil which is nearly odourless. It is said to be used medicinally. I procured three ounces of the oil from six pounds of bruised nutmegs.

Pongamia Glabra.—The seeds of this tree are collected by natives in Malabar. The oil yielded by them is thick and of a darkish colour. It is used medicinally for cutaneous affections, and is burnt by the poorer classes.

Ricinus Communis.—The castor oil shrub is too well known to need description. It is found both cultivated and wild especially on the banks of the Nelambur river. The oil is extensively manufactured in Malabar and the creaking mills in which the seed is crushed may be seen in every village in the district. The seed of this plant furnishes the food of the bronze-winged dove (*Chalcophaps Indica*).

Schleichera Trijuga.—This handsome tree is abundant in Malabar, where it is preserved for the sake of its seed, which contains a large percentage of oil. The oil is principally used for burning; but also medicinally, and in the manufacture of birdlime.

Strychnos nux vomica.—This tree is found from the sea-level to 2,500 feet in Wynaad. An oil is said to be expressed from the seeds, and used medicinally by natives. Large quantities of the seeds are exported from Calicut by the Firm of Messrs. D. Maneekji and Sons.

Tamarindus Indicus.—This tree only thrives in the Palghat Taluq, as it prefers a dry climate. The seeds produce a clear thin oil. It is for the sake of the fruit however that the tree is chiefly valued.

Tectona grandis.—The seed of the Teak tree contains a good deal of oil.

Terminalia bellerica.—The kernel of the seeds yields by expression a medicinal oil of a greenish colour. The *T. Chebula* yields a somewhat similar oil.

Vateria Malabarica.—The seeds yield by boiling a solid fat of a pale yellow colour, used for burning. It might be utilized in the manufacture of soap and candles.

Xylia dolabriformis.—The seeds are said to yield an oil.

Tan Barks and Dyes.

Acacia arabica.—The bark of this tree is occasionally used for tanning. It yields an excellent brown dye, which can be changed to black by the addition of proto-sulphate of iron, as a mordant. I have often dyed shikar suits with it, and the colour is permanent. Many of the other acacias are used for dyeing and tanning notably *A. Decurrens* an Australian species.

Albizzia Lebbek.—The bark of this tree is occasionally used for tanning.

Areca Catechu.—The nuts are used for dyeing and might be used for tanning, were they not too expensive for this purpose.

Artocarpus integrifolia.—The wood of this tree made into a decoction produces a yellow dye.

Bixa orellana.—The reddish powder that covers the seeds of this plant are used for dyeing.

Briedelia retusa.—The bark of this thorny tree can be used for tanning.

Butea frondosa.—The gaudy flowers of this tree are used for dyeing; but the colours are fleeting.

Cæsalphinia Sappan.—This small tree is most extensively cultivated throughout Malabar. It reaches a larger size in Wynaad, however, than it does on the Coast. When a daughter is born in a Thean family, the father plants a certain number of Sappan trees, which form her dowry when married. There are factories at Calicut where the dye is prepared. I found on visiting them that the wood cut into chips was boiled, and a quantity of country arrowroot was then thrown into the decoction and when saturated, removed and dried. This pink powder is exported in large quantities to the

Arabian Gulf, Cutch, &c. The Chinese pay a high price for Sappan wood when the billets are long, straight, free from flaws, and thick. This looks as if they employed the wood in turnery and cabinet work. In Malabar, however, the trees are, as a rule, poor and crooked, and are grubbed up roots and all, before they reach maturity.

Cathartocarpus (Cassia) fistula.—The bark of this tree is principally used in Malabar for tanning.

Cedrela Toona.—The flowers yield a reddish dye.

Curcuma aromatica.—Wild turmeric is found in the forests of Wynaad and the Western Ghâts. It is extensively collected and is known as "Custoory Manja." It is used by native women as a cosmetic and in dyeing.

Cynometra ramiflora.—A decoction of the chips of the heartwood of this tree yields a fine purplish dye.

Diospyros Embryopteris.—The fruit of this tree is used for tanning and dyeing. In combination with proto-sulphate of iron (Annabathy) it produces all shades of brown, brownish-black, and black.

Erythrina Indica.—The scarlet flowers of this tree produce a red dye.

Eugenia Sp.—All species of Eugenia produce barks used for tanning and dyeing. In combination with the salts of iron, all shades of brown and black can be obtained.

Lagerstrœmia microcarpa.—The bark is said to be used in tanning.

Lawsonia alba.—The young leaves of this shrub are largely used by Mahomedans for dyeing their nails, beards and horse tails occasionally—a bright orange red.

Mallotus Phillipenensis (Rottlera tinctoria).—This small tree is very abundant from the sea-coast to 2,500 feet in Wynaad. The clusters of orange-red berries are very striking in February when the berries ripen. The dye is the downy bloom that covers the fruit. It is obtained by drying the berries and shaking them smartly in a vessel when the powder is rubbed off and falls to the bottom. It is not easily soluble in water; but is completely so in alcohol. The colour is of a brilliant yellow.

Mangifera Indica.—The young fruit of the mangoe when dried is sometimes used as a mordant.

Memecylon tinctorium.—The flowers and leaves are used in dyeing in combination with other dyes.

Michelia Champaca.—The flowers of this handsome timber tree are used for dyeing a pale yellow. The blossoms are very sweet scented.

Morinda tinctoria.—This small tree is found in the Walayar Reserves, and in the forests near Palghat. The bark of the roots yields a reddish dye.

Wodina Wodier.—The bark of this tree is sometimes used for tanning.

Phyllanthus Emblica.—The fruit and leaves are used for tanning and dyeing. With gallnuts and proto-sulphate of iron, a deep and permanent black is produced. The fruit is eaten raw and pickled.

Pterocarpus marsupium.—This tree produces the gum kino of commerce. The heartwood when cut into chips and soaked in water, yields a pale-blue dye.

Randia dumetorum.—The fruit of this thorny shrub, which is common throughout Malabar, is principally used to poison fish. The bark is used medicinally, and the fruit is said to be used in dyeing.

Salix tetrasperma.—Common in swamps in the Wynaad. The bark is astringent, and would make good tan bark; but is not used in Malabar.

Semecarpus Anacardium.—The pericarp of the seed of this tree produces a black oily liquid used for marking linen in combination with quicklime as a mordant.

Soymida febrifuga.—The bark is used medicinally and in tanning.

Tectona grandis.—On crushing the young leaves of this

tree, a bright lake-coloured dye is produced. I have not heard of its being used for dyeing.

Terminalia bellerica.—The seeds of this tree are used in tanning and dyeing. Sambur and other deer eat the fruit.

Terminalia Chebula.—The gallnut tree is only found in the forests in the extreme east of Wynaad. The crop is annually leased out. The seeds and leaf galls when collected are taken to Mysore, where they are extensively used in Hunsur and Collegal in tanning leather. A solution of gallnuts with protosulphate of iron is used in the manufacture of ink. A durable black dye is obtained from a decoction of myrabolans; the cloth after being dyed, is dipped in a strong solution of proto-sulphate of iron. A yellowish brown dye is produced if the salts of iron are not used. Alum is usually used as a mordant, when it is desired to fix the shade of brown required. Gallnuts constitute one of the most important forest products of the Madras Presidency.

Fruit and Edible Roots.

Baccaurea Sapida.—The trunk of this tree is thickly covered in October with bunches of reddish-coloured fruit. The aril of the seed, which is sweet, and sub-acid is eaten, and resembles the Mangosteen in flavour. It is capable of cultivation and improvement. It is abundant in the Ghât forests.

Solanum robusta.—This handsome solanum bears clusters of orange-coloured fruit, the size of a billiard ball. The fruits are densely covered with a coarse velvetty coat of fine prickles. When the epidermis has been peeled, the fruit resembles the boiled yolk of an egg and tastes exactly like the fruit of *Physalis Peruviana*; it is very closely allied to a solanum introduced from Brazil by Mr. Broughton the Government Quinologist, some thirteen years ago; the only difference being that the stems of *S. Robusta* are armed as well as the leaves, whilst the Brazilian species is unarmed. There is no perceptible difference in the fruit.

Eugenia Species.—The fruit of all species of Eugenia is edible. The rose apple, Jamoon and others are too well known to need description. On the summits of the Western Ghâts a very beautiful species is abundant, with bright blue flowers and pear-shaped fruit, the size of a robin's egg, of a brilliant golden, or scarlet colour, and looking like drops of molten sealing wax.

Phyllanthus Emblica.—The sour and astringent fruit of this small tree is eaten raw and pickled. It possesses the peculiar property of turning brackish water sweet.

Garcinias.—The fruit of almost all the trees of this genus are edible. The Mangosteen is one of the most important. Some are eaten pickled, and some made into tarts.

Diospyros Melanoxylon.—The fruit of this tree is edible, and is occasionally sold in the bazaars.

Zizyphus Jujuba.—This tree yields a sour little orange plum, which is eaten by native boys and deer.

Spondias Mangifera.—The Hog plum—is eaten pickled by natives; it is also greedily devoured by deer, &c.

Artocarpus Integrifolia.—The fruit of this tree is eaten, when green in curries. The seeds are eaten roasted.

Ficus species.—The fruit of most trees of this genus are eaten in times of scarcity and by animals. There is a scandent species, with a trunk rarely over six inches in diameter that produces bunches of very large purple figs which, when ripe, are by no means ill-flavoured. The bright orange fruit of the common atti have a very pleasant smell; but they are usually full of thousands of small double-tailed flies. All wild animals eat the fruit of wild figs greedily. There are very few trees, or shrubs in these vast forests that bear edible fruit. It is surprising that amongst such a variety of trees there should be so few fruit-bearing ones.

Of Edible Substances other than Fruit.

Phœnix Sylvestris yields a very delicate and nutty-flavoured cabbage that is eaten both raw and pickled.

Caryota Urens also yields a cabbage and an abundance of toddy or palm wine.

Calamas Sp.—The larger rattans when cut, yield an abundance of limpid sap which is used as a substitute for water, where none is obtainable.

Termes Sp.—Not only are the perfect winged insects of this genus eaten as food by man, beast, bird, reptile and fish, but their conical dwellings often furnish a crop of excellent mushrooms of two species. The one, very small, and of a white colour, appearing in thousands in the Wynaad in June and July, and the other, as a rule, found only in the forests, of a slightly darker colour, and of larger size and excellent flavour which grows from the underground spongy masses of wood, in which the young white ants are reared. Cattle propagate a third edible species by eating the mushrooms and dropping the spawn afterwards over the grass hills in the Wynaad.

Honey and Wax are both plentiful and abundant in Malabar. The exuberance of vegetation, and millions of flowering trees, offering a fine field to the many species of these industrious little insects. There are four species of honey bees in the forests of Malabar.

Apis dorsata.—The largest of all is a fierce and irascible insect which it is highly dangerous to meddle with. It breeds on cliffs.

Apis Mellifica.—This bee is identical with the European bees, and I see no reason why it should be separated as distinct; it breeds in holes of trees, rocks, &c., is easily domesticated, and in hill regions above 3,000 feet elevation, produces the best honey.

Apis florea, is a very small bee that builds on twigs of trees, bushes, &c.; it is not capable of being domesticated nor worth it. The fourth species, a *Trigona,* is a very minute bee which builds in crevices of walls, &c. The globular cells are built of a mixture of resinous substances, which I have seen these little creatures collecting from

Mesua, Canarium, Callophyllum, Artocarpus and other trees. It resembles cobbler's wax in appearance. The amount obtainable from each hive is very small, half a pound or so. An allied species in Burmah (*Trigona lœviceps*) produces a similar substance which the Burmese use for caulking boats. The only use to which I have seen the wax of the Indian *Trigona* put, is in waterproofing the powder pan of matchlocks, and for the mouth pieces of Indian Bag-pipes which are made with too reeds and a gourd.

Silk.—There are numerous species of silk-producing moths in the Wynaad, and Malabar, the principal of which are the Tassa moth (*Antherœa paphia*). The Atlas moth (*Attacus atlas*) and the sociable silk moth (*Cricula Trifenestrata*).

Edible Roots, &c.

Dioscorea Sp.—All the Dioscoreas produce edible roots, some are cultivated, and others grow wild, and form the chief support of aboriginal tribes in the dry weather and times of scarcity. These roots are the chief mainstay of Coorumbers and others, and without them they would be wretched indeed. The women and children are sent out daily to search for, and dig up the long tuberous roots which often descend into the earth, to a depth of six or seven feet. It is a work of great labour to the poor women to excavate the holes in the baked and hardened soil to this depth. The roots when cooked in the ashes are mealy, and well-flavoured, and must contain a great deal of nourishment.

On the higher slopes of the Western Ghâts, an edible *orchis* occurs—the "salep" of the shops, which is used medicinally, and is in great repute amongst Mahomedan Doctors.

Curcuma Angustifolia yields arrowroots in large quantities which is manufactured to a considerable extent in Malabar. Other species of *Curcuma* also produce arrowroot. Most of the species are abundant in the forests of Malabar.

Piper nigrum.—Wild pepper is abundant in all the evergreen forests, and is collected to a small extent.

Chavica Betel.—This vine grows wild in the deep ravines of the Chenat Nair Forests.

Chavica Roxburghii.—The *Pipli* or long-tailed pepper is very common in the forests of Nilambur; it grows wild everywhere along the foot of the Ghâts.

Acacia Concinna.—The pods of this thorny scandent acacia form one of the most important of our forest products. They are eagerly sought for, and collected. Natives use the fruit for washing their heads.

Deer horns, Ivory, &c.—The former are picked up, and sold to merchants in February and March when the grass has been burnt. Ivory is but rarely found, and is then of but little value as it is more or less damaged from exposure and the gnawing of porcupines.

Fibres and Paper Materials.

Agave Americana—grows fairly well in Palghat; but does not occur further west. Yields a strong fibre which is manufactured into twine, hammocks, &c. It ought to yield a valuable paper stock.

Agave Vivipara.—This species replaces the former in the moisture regions of the West Coast. It furnishes an excellent fibre, closely resembling that of *A. Americana;* but the staple is not so long, the leaves being shorter.

Ananassa Sativa—grows wild in parts of Wynaad, and the Western Coast. The leaves furnish a strong and beautifully silky fibre, which is not however utilized in any way.

Artocarpus integrifolia—furnishes a strong fibre.

Bambusa Arundinacea.—The young shoots of this bamboo yield excellent paper stock. All the other species of bamboos also yield paper stock. The young shoots of *Bheesha rheedii,* and *Bheesha Travancorica* yield a superior paper stock.

Bauhinia Sp.—The bark of all the bauhinias is fibrous and yield a good bast.

Bohmeria Malabarica.—This small tree yields a magnificent silky fibre greatly valued by the Coorchias and other aboriginal tribes for bow strings on account of its great strength. It grows freely in all shola forests in the neighbourhood of water in ravines. The fibre closely resembles the rheea and might be profitably cultivated. It is known by the Coorchias under the name of Mannali. There are several other bohmerias in the Ghât forests which furnish excellent fibre.

Bohmeria nivea.—The Rheea has been introduced into the Manantoddy Botanical Garden, and has thriven there.

Bombax Malabaricum.—The silky down of this tree is largely used on the coast for stuffing pillows, &c. The fibre from the bark can be made into cordage.

Borassus flabelliformis.—The petioles of the leaves are fibrous, and can be utilised for paper or cordage.

Butea frondosa.—The bark yields a strong fibre.

Calamus Sp.—Canes and rattans are extensively used in the district. The former principally for walking sticks; those from the Anamallay forests are famous. Rattans are used for ropes across rivers and in the Wynaad in the monsoon, almost all large rivers are crossed on bamboo rafts with a loop at the head through which the rattan cable passes. By hauling the cable, the raft is gradually forced across the river. On the Anamallays deer and ibex are snared with rattan nooses. The uses to which all species of calamus are put are innumerable.

Calatropis Gigantea.—This shrub is found in Palghat. The bark yields a very strong, soft, silky, fibre used for fishing-lines, &c.

Cannabis Sativa.—Hemp is not cultivated for its fibre at all in the district. A few plants are occasionally seen near the houses of natives, who grow it solely for the intoxicating "bhang" it produces, and which is largely smoked by Mahomedans.

Careya Arborea, furnishes an excellent fibre, used by natives principally in house-building, &c.

Caryota urens.—This palm yields an exceedingly valuable fibre which is extensively used in Malabar for fishing-lines. Surrounding the base of the petioles of the leaves, there is a mass of coarse wire-like fibre, varying in thickness from the size of horse-hair to that of a knitting needle. This fibre is used in Malabar for elephant ropes, &c., but is valued at home for the manufacture of brushes, and is known to the trade by the name of Kittal fibre. From the petioles of the leaves, however, a strong yellowish fibre is drawn, which when knotted together makes excellent fishing-lines. This fibre is sometimes boiled in milk which makes it last longer the native fishermen say. It is brittle when dry; but very strong when wet and pliable. Unfortunately the cabbage of this palm is edible, and it is exterminated both by natives and wild elephants, wherever found in the forests. Were it not for this, the forests of Malabar would abound with millions of these very valuable palms. In addition to the fibre, and cabbage produced by them, the older palms contain starch from which sago is manufactured in Malabar; but it is of poor quality. The flower spathes are cut and yield large quantities of the best toddy. This palm deserves special protection.

Corypha umbraculifera.—The leaves of this handsome palm are used for an infinite variety of purposes, for thatching houses, umbrellas, the covers of bullock coaches, &c., &c.

Cyperus Corymbosus.—The very handsome Palghat mats are made from this cyperus which grows wild on the banks of streams.

Eriodendron unfructuosum.—The bark yields a fibre, which might be used for paper stock. The silky down surrounding the seeds is used for stuffing pillows.

Ficus Species.—The bark of the trunk and especially of the aerial roots of all figs yield fibre, more or less strong and suitable for cordage, paper stock, &c. The fibre of the aerial roots of *Ficus parasiticus* is highly valued in Wynaad for bow strings by the Coorchias and is there known as colinâr—not to be confounded with the coli nâr of Canara which is produced by *Helicteres isora*, a shrub.

Girardinia heterophylla.—This nettle produces an excellent fibre of great strength. It is not used in any way in the district, though the Todas of the Neilgherries extract and use it for thread.

Grewia tiliæfolia.—All the Grewias yield good fibre. Wild elephants are very fond of the bark of this species. It is sometimes used for the drag ropes of elephants.

Helicteres isora.—A common shrub in Malabar which yields an excellent fibre, largely used for the large timber drag ropes, by which elephants haul timber in Malabar. It ought to make excellent paper stock.

Hibiscus Species.—All the plants belonging to this genus are fibre producers. The most important however is one in the Wynaad, with a small pink flower, which grows in extraordinary abundance everywhere, and produces a splendid fibre, well worthy of attention *(H. procera ?)*.

Kydia Calycina.—A small tree common in the deciduous forests. The bark yields a fair fibre.

Laportea crenulata.—The bark of this unpleasant shrub yields a white strong fibre; but the stinging hairs of the petioles of the leaves cause such agony that few care to meddle with the plant.

Musa textilis.—The Manilla hemp produces a very strong and durable fibre. It has been introduced into the Wynaad and thrives there. The fibre would answer well for paper stock.

Musa ornata grows wild on the slopes of the Western Ghâts, and produces a strong but coarse fibre.

Musa Superba.—Abundant in the sholas of the Western Ghâts. The natives use the leaves for plates. The fibre is strong and durable.

Odina Wodier yields a fair bast.

Pandanus odoratissima.—The leaves are used largely on the Coast, in the manufacture of mats. They might be turned into paper stock, as well as the fibrous stems. A species of Pandanus which is found in the Cardamom forests, and which is stemless is also used for the same purposes.

Polyalthia Coffeoides.—The bark of this tree yields a good fibre, which is occasionally used for elephant drag ropes.

Sponia orientalis.—The bark of this tree yields a fibre.

Sterculia guttata.—The bark of this species yields an excellent fibre, much valued by the natives.

Sterculia urens yields a fair fibre.

Sterculia Villosa.—This is known as "Anay Vaccay Nâr" and is almost exclusively used in the manufacture of elephant drag ropes.

Yucca gloriosa grows well in the Wynaad; the leaves yield a very tough fibre.

CHAPTER XV.

FUEL PLANTATIONS.

Prize Essay*

In the Madras Presidency we have various climates and soils, and different degrees of rainfall. It stands to reason that a tree which would succeed admirably on the sandy littoral of the East Coast, would be an utter failure on the Nílgiris. We have, therefore, to take into consideration several points before starting an undertaking of this nature.

In the first place we must obtain our land in the immediate neighbourhood of the market in which we propose to sell our wood, or otherwise the cost of transporting the fuel would infallibly eat up the profits. A plentiful supply of

* By Rhodes Morgan, Esq., F.Z.S., Deputy Conservator of Forests.

cheap labour is the next requisite, and a soil suitable to the particular species of tree we wish to plant.

In our choice of the most suitable tree to plant, we must remember to choose such as will produce the greatest out-turn to the acre within a given period of time, and at the same time possesses such an amount of calorific power, as will enable it to compete successfully with slower-growing woods possessing a higher amount of latent caloric.

In Trichinopoly, I experimented with a considerable variety of fuel trees, for the supply of wood to the Railway, and judging from my own experience and that of others, the *Casuarina muricata* is far and away the best.

It will not, however, do to plant this tree in *all* soils. In a stiff clay it grows but slowly, and sometimes even dies; whereas in deep, fine sand, it distances all other fuel-trees in its rapid and surprising rate of growth.

It suits itself to a wonderful variety of climate, and fine specimens may be seen growing in the arid plains of the East Coast, the moist and humid shores of Malabar, and inland, at an elevation of 2,500 feet, at Manantoddy.

In addition to its great value as a fuel-producer, its timber is used for building purposes, and is capable of bearing a higher cross strain than almost any other known species of Indian tree.

When grown by itself, and allowed to branch, it is highly ornamental, and a desirable addition to an avenue, or park.

We will now assume that the would-be fuel-planter has obtained a block of 100 acres of suitable land within a mile of his market.

The first thing to be then done, is to obtain a sufficient number of ripe cones, gathered from the most vigorous, healthy, and mature Casuarina trees we can find, and put them in the sun to open. Care must be taken that ants do not get at the seeds, or they will destroy every one. The cones should, therefore, be placed on a table, the legs of which should be protected by being placed in tins containing kerosine oil.

The next thing to be done is to select a portion of the land obtained, for the formation of a nursery in the immediate neighbourhood of fresh water.

As Casuarina plantations should be formed only on the sandy banks of rivers, or near the seashore, water is generally to be found within a few feet of the surface. It will, therefore, be necessary to sink a well. To do this no great outlay is needed, for it is not necessary that the well should last longer than two years at the most. In Trichinopoly, in the sandy soil of the banks of the Cauvery,—there known as "Padugay" land—I found the following contrivance answer splendidly:—

I made an open cylinder of basket-work, of a creeper I found growing in the neighbourhood, resembling osier in its qualities. The cylinder, four feet in diameter by six feet in height, I placed over the spot where I wished to sink my well. A man then got into the basket and scooped away the sandy soil at the bottom, which he handed up in a vessel to men seated on the rim of the cylinder to press it down. As the soil was undermined, the basket-work sank till it became flush with the surface of the earth, when another six feet of creeper was woven on to it, and the previous process repeated. In this manner when a depth of seven feet of water had been obtained, the well was completed, and a Picottah rigged up. For about a fortnight after, the water of the well is foul and useless, owing to the putrefaction of the bark, leaves and small twigs of the creeper; but if it is daily baled out, it becomes clear and sweet again.

The nursery beds should be raised to a height of three inches and should be oblongs of fourteen feet in length by three and a half in width, with path-ways of a foot in width between each.

As the best distance to plant Casuarina is six feet by six, you will require 1,200 plants, and making an allowance of

300 more for failures, 1,500 in all per acre—or for the 100 acres one lakh and 50,000.

The seed should be sown in the beds in rows six inches apart and one-eighth of an inch deep; and as the seedlings should be planted out when nine inches high, each row of three and a half feet in length will only hold about 20 plants, two inches apart. There will then be twenty-eight rows in a fourteen feet bed—holding, by the above calculation, 560 plants.

You will, therefore, require about 268 such beds for 150,000 plants for the 100 acres; and if they are ranged in eight rows of 33½ beds each, allowing for a water-channel of one foot between each bed and three feet between each of the rows, your nursery will occupy 133 feet × 150 feet = 19,950 square feet; and allowing 400 square feet for the well and lift, a total of 20,350 square feet, or half an acre, less 136⅜ square yards—say half an acre.

The nursery should be surrounded by a stout fence, and the cheapest and best is undoubtedly a sunk fence of four feet in depth, wedge-shaped at the base, so that cattle cannot get out and over into the nursery; the inner edge of the ditch should be constructed of green croton stems of three inches in diameter by four feet high, or *Erythrina* (முருக்க மரம்) posts four feet apart, the intermediate spaces being carefully filled in with bamboo thorns lashed diagonally to cross reepers of split bamboos.

If the croton or Erythrina is put down at the beginning of the rains, it will speedily root, and such posts are not liable to the attacks of white ants as timber posts are.

(*N.B.*—Too much moisture rots Erythrina cuttings.)

Croton seeds can then be planted at intervals of 4″ all round the fence on the *inner* edge, and when they have grown up, a strong living fence will be formed.

To water the nurseries, all that is necessary is to divert the stream flowing from the picottah when it is worked into the channels provided for the purpose between the beds, and, as each channel is filled brimful, the entrance to it between the two beds to be watered is dammed up by scraping a mamotie full of earth up against the entrance. The bed on either side is then moistened by the percolation of the water through the sand of which it is mainly composed. Any portions of a bed not wetted by the percolation of water from the channels should be watered by a galvanised iron watering pot with a very fine rose; but it is even better to use a small garden engine till the plants are an inch or so high on account of the sand being washed by too heavy a stream of water into ridges, which smother some of the young plants and lay bare the roots of others. A spray of any required degree of fineness can be produced with the garden engine by placing the thumb over the nozzle and breaking up the jet.

When the plants are nine inches high, they should be removed from the beds by means of a transplanter, an instrument made of sheet iron of a semi-cylindrical shape, which takes up the young plant with a ball of earth round the roots, and thus prevents the fibres of the roots being broken or injured. The whole of the land having been pitted with holes of 18″ cube, the planting of the young Casuarinas is next proceeded with. The gardener in charge of the nursery, provided with a sufficient number of transplanters, rapidly removes the plants from the nurseries and hands over to a woman in attendance as many transplanters, filled with a plant each, as she can carry in a basket. The woman proceeds to the pits to be planted, where a man relieves her of her load and sends her back to the nursery with the last lot of transplanters he has emptied. A little girl now hands the transplanters with the plants, one by one, to the man; an assistant (boy) fills up the pit with the best soil near, and the man thrusts the transplanter and plant partially into the loose soil thrown in by his assistant, and with his hands fills in the earth all round, and putting two fingers of his left hand, one on each side of the stem of the plant, with his right withdraws the transplanter. Another woman should now follow with a watering can and give the newly-planted seedling a fair allowance of water, say, a gallon. Each plant should then be shaded for a few days with a basket made of cocoanut leaves or any suitable substitute.

The young plants will now require regular watering till they are firmly established and growing vigorously.

According to the Forest Report of 1872-73, page 68, Casuarina trees only seven years old averaged 60′ in height and 30″ in circumference at the ground. This has been very much my own experience; so I shall base my calculations accordingly, only allowing that they reach this size at eight years and not seven.

I have estimated the price of Casuarina seedlings at Rs. 6 per 1,000 at the outside. An acre of land will contain 1,200 pits 6 × 6; we will therefore allow 1,500 plants to the acre; 300 to replace failures.

Pitting should not cost more than Rs. 6 an acre as, the soil being sandy, 200 18′ cube pits can be cut for a rupee. Staking the pits ought to be done for Rs. 2 an acre; if this is not neatly done, the work will not look shipshape.

Planting, watering, and shading for the first week I put down at Rs. 9 an acre.

The subsequent watering till the plants are established will cost Rs. 26 an acre at least.

Fencing ought not to cost more than Rs. 3 an acre. Replanting failures and sundries, one rupee. Quit-rent at one rupee an acre will be Rs. 8 up to the period when the crop is fit to fell.

Taking eight-year old trees to contain on an average 10 cubic feet all round, and, supposing that only 1,000 such trees survive out of the 1,200 planted, we have 10,000 cubic feet of wood, and as Casuarina weighs about 60lb. green to the cubic foot, 600,000lb. of fuel (÷ 2,240), or 267$\frac{6}{7}$ tons.

The average selling price of such fuel is Rs. 8 per ton; therefore the sum realised will be Rs. 2,142-13-8.

Interest on the outlay incurred will amount at 10 per cent., to, on Rs. 64, Rs. 6-6-5 per annum.

Felling and sawing into billets at five annas per tree, Rs. 312-8-0.

Carting 267$\frac{6}{7}$ tons at Rs. 1-4-0 per ton = Rs. 334-13-1.

Supervision and Sundries Rs. 80.

Our account now stands thus :—

A.

Expenditure.	RS.	A.	P.	Receipts.	RS.	A.	P.
1,500 plants at Rs. 6 per 1,000 plants	9	0	0	Sum realised by sale of 267$\frac{6}{7}$ tons of fuel	2,142	13	8
Pitting	6	0	0	Deduct Expenditure...	842	8	5
Staking and Lining ...	2	0	0				
Planting, Watering, Shading (one week) ...	9	0	0	Profit...	1,300	5	3
Watering till the plants are established ...	26	0	0				
Fencing	3	0	0				
Replanting failures ...	1	0	0				
Quit-rent	8	0	0				
Total...	64	0	0				
Interest at 10 per cent. on above	51	3	4				
Felling and sawing into billets—1,000 trees at five annas per tree ...	312	8	0				
Carting 267$\frac{6}{7}$ tons at Rs. 1-4-0 per ton ...	334	13	1				
Supervision and Sundries	80	0	0				
Grand Total of Expenditure	842	8	5				

A Casuarina plantation can also be worked as a mixed fuel and timber plantation, a percentage of the finest trees being left to the acre after the smaller ones have been thinned out; but, as this essay is entirely on fuel plantations, I will not enter further into the subject.

In addition to Casuarina, there is a considerable variety of indigenous and of introduced trees that yield the finest fuel.

I append the following list of a few such :—

Acacia Arabica ...	Karu-Veylum ...	கருவேலம்.
,, leucophlœa	Vel-Veylum ...	வெள்வேலம்.
Cassia floribunda..	Konnay	கொண்ணை.
Albizzia lebbeck...	Vaghay	வாகே.
Acacia amara ...	Woonjal	ஊஞ்சல்.
Inga dulcis	Korkapilly	கொருக்காபுளி.
And many others.		

In addition to producing good fuel of high calorific power, the *Acacia Arabica* and *Albizzia lebbeck* produce timber of considerable value, the dense dark-red heart-wood being used for a variety of economical purposes.

The black heart-wood of *Cassia floribunda* is also a valuable wood.

If, in obtaining a block of 100 acres of land, a portion is found unfitted for Casuarina, it is advisable to plant any or all of the above mentioned species of fuel-producing woods, which in a stiff soil, like black cotton, are almost certain to produce a heavier outturn per acre within the same period of time.

It is a mistake to thin out a portion or the whole of a fuel or timber plantation and replant the places occupied by the trees so taken out. Not only will the trees left standing be detrimental to the young plants from the shade cast by their branches, but their roots will deprive the little ones of all nourishment and kill them.

It is far better to fell over completely a portion or the whole of the block and allow the stools to shoot up into coppice, when the coppice may again be felled when it has reached a sufficient size; but the outturn will be a little less than the original crop taken off the land, within the same period of time previously.

With Casuarina not more than three or four coppicings can with advantage be effected on the same land, it being preferable to replant for the fourth crop with another species of tree if possible; but, if the land is sandy—and all land selected for Casuarina is mostly so—other species will make but poor growth, unless such sandy land is situated on the bank of a river, where I have found that the trees previousily mentoned will succeed.

Fuel Plantations on the Nilgiris.

The Australian trees introduced into the Nílgiris are by far the best to plant for fuel purposes. The indigenous species of fuel-trees cannot, in any way, be compared with them, as they are, one and all, so very slow in their rates of growth compared to the introduced trees.

Though many species of Eucalyptus have been introduced, *E. Globulus* has taken most kindly to the soil, and has produced the most astonishing results. The two Australian Acacias, *Melanoxylon* and *Dealbata*, are both excellent, especially the flowering Acacia or Wattle of the Australian Colonists, and are of quick growth. *Melanoxylon*, in addition to its producing good fuel, is an excellent timber, known in Australia as blackwood, and much used and valued there.

On the Nílgiris many of the indigenous sholas have been utterly destroyed in order to create fuel plantations of the above three species of trees, and this is a shame, for the Eucalyptus, especially, thrives exceedingly well on grass land, though not so well as on shola, and the Acacias, *Melanoxylon* and *Dealbata*, also succeed in grass-land, especially in rich hollows.

The thousands of acres of grass-lands in the immediate neighbourhood of Ootacamund, if planted up with a mixture of *E. Globulus* and Acacias would have supplied the whole of the fuel requirements of Ootacamund for ever.

The * Wattle has the habit of throwing out suckers from the roots, often at a distance of seventy yards from the main stem, in surprising numbers; and a single tree will, in a few

* A *Melanoxylon* does the same; but not so freely.

years, surround itself with thousands of smaller ones if planted by itself, especially if a ditch one foot deep is cut *through* the roots at a distance of twenty or thirty yards from the stem, and afterwards other concentric rings are cut within and without the first one at intervals of six feet. Every root severed will throw up suckers. In grass-land, wattle might be sown broadcast, after ploughing up the ground carefully. Seed can be obtained on the hills at about three annas per pound. It should be sown, like wheat or barley, on soil well pulverised by frequent ploughings and thoroughly saturated by the early monsoon showers, and then harrowed in. As this system has never been tried, to my knowledge, on the hills, I merely throw this out as a suggestion. The seedlings should grow up exactly like the sucker crop that succeeds a clean felling of wattle, and must be treated the same way, the produce will be about equal to a sucker crop. In making a fuel plantation of the wattle all that is necessary is to plant the land up with seedlings 12 feet × 6 feet, in holes two feet cube, dropping a few seeds in as well into each hole, for the greater the number of *roots* the better and sooner will the plantation get on. This should be done in June, when the south-west monsoon bursts, and in cloudy weather. If the plantation is carefully protected from cattle,—for goats eat the leaves greedily—the first crop will be ready to fell at the end of the seventh year, and each tree will produce, on an average, including the branches, about ten cubic feet of wood, weighing at 60lbs. per cubic foot about 600lbs. or a total of 360,000lbs. per acre, calculating 600 trees to the acre at 12 feet × 6 feet. This would produce about 160 tons and valued at 8 Rupees per ton, Rs. 1,280.

The cost of cartage would come to about Rs. 320 at two rupees per ton, for it cannot be done cheaper on the hills, where rates are rather dear—and even if the plantation were not more than a mile from the market.

The cost of pitting would be about Rs. 7-8 per acre of planting Rs. 2.

The plants would not cost more than Rs. 1-8, as they will grow with very little care and trouble, and the seed can be sown broadcast. Seed would cost eight annas.

The rent would come to Rs. 14 for the seven years at Rs. 2 per acre. Watchman's charges would not exceed Rs. 1-8 per year or Rs. 4-8 per acre for three years, when the young trees will be past danger. The following balance sheet will show the profit approximately to be expected on a Wattel Plantation :—

B.

Expenditure.	RS.	A.	P.	Receipts.	RS.	A.	P.
600 plants and 1 lb. of seed ...	2	0	0	By sale of 160 tons of fuel at Rs. 8 per ton	1,280	0	0
Pitting 600 pits at Rs. 1-4 per 100	7	8	0	Deduct expenditure.	616	0	0
Watchman for 3 years ...	4	8	0	Profit, Rs.	664	0	0
Planting 600 plants	2	0	0				
Quit-rent	14	0	0				
Total ...	30	0	0				
Interest at 10 per cent. on above, for 7 years ...	21	0	0				
Felling and lopping 600 trees at 6 annas per tree ...	225	0	0				
Carting 160 tons at Rs. 2 per ton	320	0	0				
Supervision and sundries ...	20	0	0				
Grand Total ...	616	0	0				

INDEX.